THE CLOUD
OF UNKNOWING

Foreword by Tim Farrington

Edited by Emilie Griffin

HarperOne
A Division of HarperCollins*Publishers*

HarperOne

HarperCollins books may be purchased for educational, business, or sales promotional use. For information please write: Special Markets Department, HarperCollins Publishers, 10 East 53rd Street, New York, NY 10022.

HarperCollins Web site: http://www.harpercollins.com
HarperCollins®, ♦®, and HarperOne™ are trademarks of HarperCollins Publishers.

Book Design by Susan Rimerman

Library of Congress Cataloging-in-Publication Data
The cloud of unknowing. — 1st ed.
    p. cm.
  ISBN: 978-0-06-073775-7
    1. Mysticism—Early works to 1800.   I. HarperSanFrancisco (Firm)
BV5082.3.C5   2004
248.2'2—dc22   2004056845

07 08 09 10 11 RRD(H) 10 9 8 7 6 5 4 3

CONTENTS

FOREWORD

I first stumbled upon *The Cloud of Unknowing* in the spring of 1983, in what amounted to a master stroke of divine irony, in the library of the Siddha Yoga Ashram in Oakland, California. I had abandoned my native Catholicism for Zen Buddhism some ten years earlier; my capricious teenage Buddhism had led me to California; and the vagaries of the Bay Area's eclectic spiritual clearinghouse had, by various incongruous means (including a waitress with whom I would have liked to have slept), brought me to the converted fleabag hotel at the corner of Stanford and San Pablo Avenue, where devotees of Swami Muktananda practiced a species of Kundalini yoga.

I had been in the ashram for a year by then, absorbed in its Hindu monastic routine, but after a honeymoon of numinous experiences and intimations of salvation, my assiduous chanting and meditation had led me into a spiritual wilderness so vast that I was finally, at twenty-six, experiencing my fundamental cluelessness with sufficient vividness to begin to cut the crap.

I think the tiny ashram library had once been a janitor's closet. The collection was small, but dense with Patanjali, Ramana Maharshi, and such hard-core texts of the ashram's Kashmir Shaivite philosophy as the *Shiva Sutras* and *Spanda Karika*, with footnotes in Sanskrit. But East and West had ceased to matter to me by then; I was experiencing genuine spiritual bankruptcy and ransacking those shelves for anything remotely relevant to my straits. I certainly didn't pick up *The Cloud of Unknowing* because it is one of the classics of the Christian prayer tradition; I picked it up because the title rang true to me. God works in mysterious ways, but I had avoided the word "God" and what I considered its inevitable baggage for almost a decade by then.

What I found in the homely succinctness of *The Cloud of Unknowing* was the unmistakable voice of someone who had experienced "God" beyond all baggage and dispute. The anonymous author of the *Cloud* is not a theologian; he is a practicing contemplative, addressing a contemplative beginner, and his concern throughout the letters that compose the book is always the realities of the life of deep prayer. Writing at a time when an imprecise statement of Christian orthodoxy could still get one killed, he is careful to qualify his positions, yet his treatments of the depths of God are still breathtakingly radical—and still provoke a certain amount of academic hand-wringing—more than six centuries later. Countering the classic Augustinian view of recollection as a finding and worshiping of God "within yourself," for instance, he says: "My counsel is to take care that you are in no sense within yourself. To put it briefly, I would have you be neither outside yourself, above yourself, nor behind, nor on one side or the other." If this strikes his mentee as leaving one "nowhere" to go, then so much the better. "Leave aside this everywhere and this everything, in exchange for this nowhere and this nothing. Never mind at all if your senses have no understanding of this nothing; it is for this reason that I love it so much the better." A century earlier, Marguerite Porété was burned at the stake in downtown Paris for too exuberant a celebration of God's nothingness; and Meister Eckhart's explorations of the nowhere of "the God beyond 'God'" had also elicited the condemnation of the church. But the author of the Cloud is prepared to insist: "A person's heart is remarkably changed in the spiritual experience of this nothing when it is achieved nowhere."

The author of the Cloud is not at all blithe about the dangers of this wilderness of God— much of the book is devoted to the real dangers, pitfalls, dead ends, and delusions of the contemplative life. But he had survived it and learned to live in it. What he offers to those who wish to follow him there is not a map, for here maps give out; it is simply and deeply a way of being: "Lift up your heart to God with a humble impulse of love, and have himself as your aim, not any of his goods. . . . Set yourself to rest in this darkness. . . , always crying out after him whom you love. For if you are to experience him or to see him at all, insofar as it is possible here, it must always be in this cloud and in this darkness."

I will never forget that Oakland spring. It was cold when the fog rolled across the San Francisco Bay and hot in the East Bay when the sun burned it off. The cherry trees along San Pablo Avenue were flush with pink blossoms. I rose for meditation at four in the morning, then chopped onions for a couple hours before a quick breakfast and the daily chanting of the Guru Gita. My wardrobe consisted of a few dun and khaki T-shirts and some orange and blue University of Virginia sweatpants, my closest approach to the saffron robes of a sadhu, or ascetic. But in the afternoons I would slip away to the library instead of napping and read The Cloud of Unknowing with a mounting sense of excitement. The Cloud would eventually lead me to the more intricate nowhere of Eckhart, and to John of the Cross's sophisticated theology of the soul's dark night; but it was thanks to The Cloud of Unknowing that I truly began to make my peace with the unfathomable darkness of God. "Work hard in this nothing and this nowhere," the author of the Cloud tells us, and I was able to go on with that work and to survive the crisis of my first encounter with that nothing, in that nowhere, largely because of the simplicity, courage, and lucidity of his counsel.

For those rooted in the Christian contemplative tradition, the Cloud has long been one of the classic guides. Those practicing other forms of contemplation will find it refreshingly sage and savvy on the universal truths of the meditative life. And for prodigals like myself, who struck out overland from their Christian home country in the belief that the Western tradition held no viable meditative approaches to the depths of God, The Cloud of Unknowing may well serve, as it did for me, as a revelation, a grace, and an occasion of unspeakable gratitude.

—TIM FARRINGTON

THE CLOUD OF
UNKNOWING

PROLOGUE

In the name of the Father and of the Son and of the Holy Spirit.
Amen.

To you, whoever you are, who may have this book in your possession, whether as owner or custodian, conveyor or borrower: I lay this charge upon you and implore you with all the power and force that the bond of charity can command. You are not to read it yourself or to others or to copy it, nor are you to allow it so to be read in private or in public or copied willingly and deliberately, insofar as this is possible, except by someone or to someone who, as far as you know, has resolved with steadfast determination, truly and sincerely, to be a perfect follower of Christ; and this not only in the active life, but in the contemplative life, at the highest point which a perfect soul in this present life can possibly reach, with the help of grace, while it still dwells in this mortal body. He will be one who is doing all that he can, and has been, presumably, for a long time past, to fit himself for the contemplative life by the virtues and exercises of the active life. Otherwise this book is not for him.

I lay a further charge on you, and ask it of you with the authority of charity. If any such people do read it to themselves or to others, copy it, or else hear it read in private or in public, you must bid them, as I do you, to take time to read it in private or out loud, copy it, or listen to it right through. For it may happen that there is something there, in the beginning or in the middle, which depends on what follows and is not fully explained in that place. If so, it will be explained a little later on or else by the end. Thus if a man looks at one part and not another, he could quite easily be led into error. It is to avoid such errors, both for yourself and for anyone else, that I beg you of your charity to do as I say.

As for the worldly chatterboxes, who brazenly flatter or censure themselves or others, the rumormongers, the gossips, the tittle-tattlers, and the faultfinders of every sort, I would not want them ever to see this book. It was never my intention to write on these matters for them. I would refuse to have them interfering with it, those clever clerics, or layfolk either. For no matter how excellent they may be in matters pertaining to the active life, my subject is not for them. We must make an exception for those whose exterior state belongs to the active life and yet, because they are inwardly moved through the hidden Spirit of God, whose decisions none can read, they are enabled by an abundance of grace to share in the work of contemplation at the highest level; not of course continually, as is proper to true contemplatives, but every now and then. If men like these read this book, it should by God's grace be a great source of strength for them.

The book is divided into seventy-five chapters, and the very last sets out particular indications by which a person can find out by experience whether or not he is called by God to exercise himself in this work of contemplation.

Prelude

My spiritual friend in God: I pray and beseech you to pay very close attention to the progress of your vocation and the way in which you have been called; thank God from your heart, so that through the help of his grace you may stand steadfast in the state, degree, and manner of life that you have undertaken with full deliberation, in spite of all the subtle attacks of your bodily and ghostly enemies [cf. Eph. 6:10–13], and so win through to the crown of life [James 1:12] that lasts forever. Amen.

Chapter 1

The four degrees of the Christian life;
and how he for whom this book was
written advanced in his vocation.

My spiritual friend in God, you are to understand that,
according to our rather crude reckoning, there are four degrees
and forms of the Christian life. They are: ordinary, special, singular, and perfect. Three of these can be begun and ended in this
life [laypeople, clerics, contemplatives—ed.]; and one may
begin the fourth by grace here below, which is to last without
end in the happiness of heaven. These degrees are set out here in
order, successively, first ordinary, then special, after that singular, and finally perfect. It is in this same way, I think, according
to this very order and progress, that our Lord has, in his great
mercy, called you and led you to him by the desire of your
heart.

First, then, you are well aware that once you lived in the ordinary degree of the Christian life in the world with your friends.
And I believe that the everlasting love of the Godhead, through
which he made you and fashioned you when you were nothing
and then bought you at the price of his precious blood when, in
Adam, you were lost, would not allow you to be so far away from
him in the manner and state of your living. And so with his great
grace he kindled your desire and fastened to it a leash of longing,
and with this he led you into a more special state and degree of

life, to be a servant of the special servants of his, where you could learn to live in his service more particularly and more spiritually than you did before or could do in the ordinary way of life. What is more, it appeared that he was not going to leave you alone so easily, because of the love in his heart which he has always had for you since you first existed. What is it that he did? Do you not see with what love and with what grace he has called you up to the third degree and manner of life, which is called singular? And in this state and manner of life of the solitary you are to learn to lift up the foot of your love and step outwards toward that state and degree of life that is perfect, the last state of all.

Chapter 2

A short exhortation to humility and to
the exercise described in this book.

Look up now, feeble creature, and see what you are. What are
you, and how have you deserved to be called by our Lord? A
weary and wretched heart, indeed, is one fast asleep in sloth
which is not awakened by the drawing power of his love and the
voice of his calling! It is time, too, wretched man, to have a care
of your enemy. Do not consider yourself holier or better simply
because of the value of this vocation and because of the singular
state of life in which you find yourself. You are to consider yourself even more wretched and accursed, unless by grace and by
direction you do all that in you lies to live according to your calling. You are to be as meek and as loving to your spiritual spouse,
that is, to almighty God, the King of Kings and Lord of Lords, as
he is himself. For it was his desire to humble himself, so as to be
on a level with you, and out of the whole flock of his sheep it
was his will graciously to choose you to be one of his special
disciples. And then he brought you into this place of pasture,
where you may be fed with the sweetness of his love; all this is a
pledge of your heritage, the kingdom of heaven [cf. Song of Sol.
1:6; 2:16; Rom. 3:11; 1 Tim. 6:15; Phil. 2:6–8; Ezek. 34; Ps. 23].

Press on then with speed, I pray you. Look ahead now and
never mind what is behind [Phil. 3:13–14]; see what you still
need, and not what you have, for this is how meekness is most

quickly won and defended. Now you have to stand in desire, all your life long, if you are to make progress in the way of perfection. This desire must always be at work in your will, by the power of almighty God and by your own consent. One point I must emphasize: he is a jealous lover and allows no other partnership, and he has no wish to work in your will unless he is there alone with you, by himself. He asks no help, but only you yourself. His will is that you should simply gaze at him and leave him to act alone. Your part is to keep the windows and the door against the inroads of flies and enemies. And if you are willing to do this, all that is required of you is to woo him humbly in prayer, and at once he will help you. Call upon him then, and let us see how you get on. He is always most willing and is only waiting for you [cf. Matt. 11:28]. So what are you going to do? How will you move him?

Chapter 3

How this exercise is to be made; how it
is worth more than all other exercises.

Lift up your heart to God with a humble impulse of love, and
have himself as your aim, not any of his goods. Take care that you
avoid thinking of anything but himself, so that there is nothing
for your reason or your will to work on except himself. Do all
that in you lies to forget all the creatures that God ever made and
their works, so that neither your thought nor your desire be
directed or extended to any of them, neither in general nor in
particular. Let them alone and pay no attention to them. This is
the work of the soul that pleases God most [cf. Ps. 45:10–11]. All
saints and angels take joy in this exercise and are anxious to help
it on with all their might. All the devils are furious when you
undertake it and make it their business, insofar as they can, to
destroy it. We cannot know how wonderfully all people dwelling
on earth are helped by this exercise. Yes, and the souls in purgatory are eased of their pain, and you yourself are purified and
made virtuous, much more by this work than by any other. Yet it
is the easiest exercise of all and most readily accomplished when
a soul is helped by grace in this felt desire; otherwise, it would
be extraordinarily difficult for you to make this exercise.

Do not hang back then, but labor in it until you experience the
desire. For when you first begin to undertake it, all that you find is
a darkness, a sort of cloud of unknowing; you cannot tell what it is,

except that you experience in your will a simple reaching out to God. This darkness and cloud is always between you and your God, no matter what you do, and it prevents you from seeing him clearly by the light of understanding in your reason and from experiencing him in sweetness of love in your affection. So set yourself to rest in this darkness as long as you can, always crying out after him whom you love. For if you are to experience him or to see him at all, insofar as it is possible here, it must always be in this cloud and in this darkness. So if you labor at it with all your attention as I bid you, I trust, in his mercy, that you will reach this point.

Chapter 4

The brief nature of this exercise; it cannot be attained by intellectual study or
through the imaginative faculty.

To prevent you from making mistakes in this exercise and from thinking that it is other than it actually is, I am going to tell you a little more about it, as I believe it to be. It is an exercise that does not need a long time before it can be truly done, as some men seem to think, for it is the shortest possible of all exercises that men can imagine. It is neither longer nor shorter than an atom. The atom, if we follow the definition of good philosophers in the science of astronomy, is the smallest particle of time. It is so little that, because of its littleness, it is indivisible and almost unperceivable. It is the time of which it is written: "All time is given to you; it shall be asked of you how you have spent it." And it is right that you should give account of it, for it is neither longer nor shorter but exactly equal to each single stirring that is in the chief working power of your soul, that is, your will. For as many choices and desires, no more and no less, as there can be and are in your will in one hour, so are there atoms in an hour. If you were reformed by grace according to the primal state of man's soul as it was before sin, you would always, by the help of that grace, be in control of that impulse or of those impulses. None of them would go unheeded, but all would reach out to the preeminent and supreme object of your will and your desire, which is God himself.

He fits himself exactly to our souls by adapting his Godhead to them; and our souls are fitted exactly to him by the worthiness of our creation after his image and his likeness [Gen. 1:27]. He, by himself alone, and no one but he, is fully sufficient, and much more so to fulfill the will and the desire of our souls. And our soul, because of his reforming grace, is wholly enabled to comprehend by love the whole of him who is incomprehensible to every created knowing power, that is, to the souls of angels and of men. I speak of their knowing and not of their loving; that is why I call their souls in this case knowing powers.

Now, all rational creatures, angels and men alike, have in them, each one individually, one chief working power which is called a knowing power and another chief working power called a loving power; and of these two powers, God, who is the maker of them, is always incomprehensible to the first, the knowing power. But to the second, which is the loving power, he is entirely comprehensible in each one individually; insomuch that one loving soul of itself, because of love, would be able to comprehend him who is entirely sufficient, and much more so without limit, to fill all the souls of men and angels that could ever exist. This is the everlastingly wonderful miracle of love, which shall never have an end. For he shall ever work it and shall never cease to do so. Let him understand it who can do so by grace; for the experience of this is endless happiness, and its contrary is endless suffering.

If a man were so reformed by grace as to have constant control of the impulses of the will, he would never be without some taste of that everlasting sweetness in this life [cf. Ps. 34:8; 1 Pet. 2:3] or without the full food in the happiness of heaven [cf. Wis. 16:20]; it is his nature never to be without these impulses. So do not be surprised if I am urging you to this work. This is the exercise, as you shall hear later on, in which man would have persevered if he had never sinned. Man was made for this working, and all other things for his sake [cf. Gen. 1:28–30], to help him and speed him on to it. By this exercise he is to be restored; and for want of it, he falls deeper and deeper into sin and farther and farther from God. By perseverance and continual working in this exercise alone, without anything else, a man continues to rise higher and higher away from sin and nearer and nearer to God.

So take good care of time, therefore, and how you spend it. Nothing is more precious than time. In one small particle of time, little as it is, heaven can be won and lost. This is a sign that time is precious: God, who is the giver of time, never gives two particles of time together, but one after the other. This is because he refuses to reverse the order and the regular chain of causes in his creation. Time is made for man, not man for time [cf. Mark 2:27]. Therefore God, who is the ruler of nature, in giving time refuses to anticipate the natural impulse in a man's soul, which is exactly equal to one particle of time. So it is that man will have no excuse before God at the judgment and at the giving of the account of spending of time; he will not be able to say, "You gave two times at once and I have only one impulse at once."

Now, I hear you say sorrowfully: "How shall I fare? Since what you say is true, how shall I give an account of each particle of time separately, I who am now twenty-four years of age and never up to this day did I take heed of time? If I am to make amends now, as you well know because of what you have just written, this cannot be in any natural way or through any ordinary grace that I should be able to control, or make satisfaction for, any more particles of time than for those that are yet to come. Yes, and more than that. I am well aware, by experience, that of the times that are to come I shall no more be able to have control of one out of a hundred because of my great frailty and spiritual slowness. My reasoning is irrefutable. Help me now for the love of Jesus."

This "for the love of Jesus" is very well said. For there in the love of Jesus is your help. Love is so powerful that it makes everything ordinary. So love Jesus, and everything that he has is yours [cf. Luke 15:31]. By his Godhead he is the maker and giver of time. By his manhood he is truly the keeper of time. And by his Godhead and manhood together he is the truest judge and accountant of the spending of time. Knit yourself, then, to him by love and by faith. And in virtue of that knot you shall be a regular partner with him and with all who are so well fastened to him by love; that is, with our Lady, St. Mary, who was full of all grace in the keeping of time [cf. Luke 1:28], and with all the angels of heaven that can never lose time, and with all the saints in heaven and on earth, who by the grace of Jesus keep time in perfect justice because of love.

Look and see what comfort there is here. Understand it as a theologian would, and get profit from it. But one warning I give you above all others: I cannot see who may truly claim this fellowship with Jesus and his holy mother, his high angels and also with his saints, unless he be such a man that does all that in him lies with the help of grace to value time, so that he may be seen to be one who makes a profit on his part, little as this is, for the whole fellowship, as each of the others does on theirs.

Pay careful heed, then, to this exercise and to the wonderful way in which it works within your soul. For when rightly understood, it is nothing else than a sudden impulse, one that comes without warning, speedily flying up to God as the spark flies up from the burning coal. Marvelous also are the number of such impulses that can take place in one hour in a soul that is properly disposed for the exercise. Yet in one stirring out of all these, a man can suddenly and perfectly have forgotten every created thing. And equally quickly, after each impulse, because of the corruption of the flesh, the soul falls down again to some thought or some deed done or undone. But what matter? For straightaway it rises again as suddenly as it did before.

In this, then, one can quickly understand the way of this working and realize clearly that it is far removed from any fancy or false imagination or subtle opinion; for all these are brought about not by that devout and humble simple impulse of love, but by a proud, speculative, and overimaginative reasoning. These proud and elaborate speculations must always be pushed down and heavily trodden underfoot, if this exercise is to be truly understood in purity of spirit.

Whoever hears this exercise read or spoken of may think that he can or ought to achieve it by intellectual labor. And so he sits and racks his brains how it can be achieved; and with such ingenious reasonings he does violence to his imagination, perhaps beyond its natural ability, so as to fashion a false way of working which fits neither body nor soul. Truly such a man, whoever he be, is perilously deluded. And so much so that, unless God in his great goodness show him his wondrous mercy and quickly lead him away from his imaginings to put himself meekly under direction of those experienced in the exercise, he shall be overcome by frenzies or else fall into other great mischief, spiritual sins, and the devil's deceits; and through these he may easily be robbed of body and soul for all eternity. So for the love of God, take care in this exercise and do not labor with your senses or with your imagination in any way at all. For I tell you truly, this exercise cannot be achieved by their labor; so leave them and do not work with them.

Now, when I call this exercise a darkness or a cloud, do not think that it is a cloud formed out of the vapors which float in the air or a darkness such as you have in your house at night when your candle is out. For such a darkness or such a cloud you can certainly imagine by subtle fancies, as though it were before your eyes, even on the clearest day of summer; and likewise, on the darkest night of winter, you can imagine a clear shining light. But leave such falsehood alone. I mean nothing of that sort. When I say "darkness," I mean a privation of knowing, just as whatever you do not know or have forgotten is dark to you, because you do not see it with your spiritual eyes. For this reason, that which is between you and your God is termed not a cloud of the air, but a cloud of unknowing.

Chapter 5

During this exercise, all creatures and
all the works of creatures, past, present,
or future, must be hidden in the cloud
of forgetting.

If ever you come to this cloud and live and work in it as I bid
you, just as this cloud of unknowing is above you, between you
and your God, in the same way you must put beneath you a
cloud of forgetting between you and all the creatures that have
ever been made. It seems to you, perhaps, that you are very far
from him, because this cloud of unknowing is between you
and your God. However, if you give it proper thought, you are
certainly much farther away from him when you do not have
the cloud of forgetting between you and all the creatures that
have ever been made. Whenever I say "all the creatures that have
ever been made," I mean not only the creatures themselves, but
also all their works and circumstances. I make no exceptions,
whether they are bodily creatures or spiritual, nor for the state
or activity of any creature, whether these be good or evil. In
short, I say that all should be hid under the cloud of forgetting.

For though it is very profitable on some occasions to think of
the state and activities of certain creatures in particular, nevertheless in this exercise it profits little or nothing. Being mindful or
thinking of any creature that God ever made, or of any of their

works either, is a sort of spiritual light. The eye of your soul is opened on it and fixed upon it, like the eye of the bowman upon the eye of the target that he is shooting at. I have one thing to say to you: everything that you think of is above you during this time, and between you and your God. Insofar as there is anything in your mind except God alone, in that far you are farther from God.

Yes, and if one may say it courteously and fittingly, in this exercise it is of little or no profit to think of the kindness or the worthiness of God, or of our Lady or the saints or angels in heaven, or even of the joys of heaven; that is to say, with a special concentration upon them, as though you wished by that concentration to feed and increase your purpose. I believe that it would in no wise be so in this case and in this exercise, for though it is good to think of the kindness of God and to love him and to praise him for that, yet it is far better to think upon his simple being and to love him and praise him for himself.

Chapter 6

A short appreciation of this exercise by
means of question and answer.

But now you put me a question and say: "How might I think of
him in himself, and what is he?" And to this I can only answer
thus: "I have no idea." For with your question you have brought
me into that same darkness, into that same cloud of unknowing, where I would you were yourself. For a man may, by grace,
have the fullness of knowledge of all other creatures and their
works, yes, and of the works of God's own self, and he is well
able to reflect on them. But no man can think of God himself.
Therefore, it is my wish to leave everything that I can think of
and choose for my love the thing that I cannot think. Because he
can certainly be loved, but not thought. He can be taken and
held by love, but not by thought. Therefore, though it is good at
times to think of the kindness and worthiness of God in particular, and though this is a light and a part of contemplation, nevertheless, in this exercise it must be cast down and covered over
with a cloud of forgetting. You are to step above it stalwartly but
lovingly, and with a devout, pleasing, impulsive love strive to
pierce that darkness above you. You are to smite upon that thick
cloud of unknowing with a sharp dart of longing love. Do not
leave that work for anything that may happen.

Chapter 7

How to deal with all thoughts during this exercise, particularly those which result from one's own investigation, knowledge, and natural acumen.

If any thought should rise and continue to press in above you and between you and that darkness, and should ask you and say, "What do you seek and what would you have?" you must say that it is God whom you would have. "Him I covet, him I seek, and nothing but him." And if the thought should ask you who that God is, you must answer that it is the God who made you and ransomed you and with his grace has called you to his love. And say, "You have no part to play." So say to the thought, "Go down again." Tread it down quickly with an impulse of love, even though it seems to you to be very holy, even though it seems that it could help you to seek him.

Perhaps the thought will bring to your mind a variety of excellent and wonderful instances of his kindness; it will say that he is most sweet and most loving, gracious and merciful. The thought will want nothing better than that you should listen to it; for in the end it will increase its chattering more and more until it brings you lower down to the recollection of his Passion. There it will let you see the wonderful kindness of God; it looks for nothing better than that you should listen to it. For soon after that it will let you see your former wretched state of life; and perhaps as you see and think upon it, the thought will bring to your mind some place in which you used to live. And so at the end, before you are even aware of it, your concentration is gone, scattered about you know not where. The cause of this dissipation is that in the beginning you deliberately listened to the thought, answered it, took it to yourself, and let it continue unheeded.

Yet what it said was nonetheless both good and holy. Yes, indeed, so holy that if any man or woman should think to come to contemplation without many sweet meditations of this sort on their own wretched state, on the Passion, on the kindness and the great goodness and the worthiness of God, they will certainly be deceived and fail in their purpose. At the same time, those men and women who are long practiced in these meditations must leave them aside, put them down, and hold them far under the cloud of forgetting, if they are ever to pierce the cloud of unknowing between them and their God.

Therefore, when you set yourself to this exercise and experience by grace that you are called by God to it, then lift up your heart to God by a humble impulse of love, and mean the God who made you and ransomed you and has in his grace called you to this exercise. Have no other thought of God; and not even any of these thoughts unless it should please you. For a simple reaching out directly toward God is sufficient, without any other cause except himself.

If you like, you can have this reaching out wrapped up and enfolded in a single word. So as to have a better grasp of it, take just a little word, of one syllable rather than of two, for the shorter it is, the better it is in agreement with this exercise of the spirit. Such a one is the word "God" or the word "love." Choose which one you prefer or any other according to your liking—the word of one syllable that you like best. Fasten this word to your heart, so that whatever happens, it will never go away. This word is to be your shield and your spear, whether you are riding in peace or in war. With this word you are to beat upon this cloud and this darkness above you. With this word you are to strike down every kind of thought under the cloud of forgetting, so that if any thought should press upon you and ask you what you would have, answer it with no other word but with this one. If the thought should offer you, out of its great learning, to analyze that word for you and to tell you its meanings, say to the thought that you want to keep it whole and not taken apart or unfastened. If you will hold fast to this purpose, you may be sure that the thought will not stay for very long. And why? Because you will not allow it to feed itself on the sort of sweet meditations that we mentioned before.

Chapter 8

An accurate treatment, by question and
answer, of certain doubts that may arise
during this exercise; the suppression of
rational investigation, knowledge, and
intellectual acumen; distinguishing the
various levels and divisions of the active
and contemplative lives.

But now you will ask, "What is this thought that presses upon
me in this work, and is it a good or an evil thing?" "If it is an evil
thing," you say, "then I am very much surprised, because it serves
so well to increase a man's devotion; and at times I believe that it
is a great comfort to listen to what it has to say. For I believe that
sometimes it can make me weep very bitterly out of compassion
for Christ in his Passion, and sometimes for my own wretched
state, and for many other reasons. All these, it seems to me, are
very holy and do me much good. And therefore I believe that
these thoughts can in no way be evil; and if it is good, and their
sweet tales do me so much good, then I am very surprised why
you bid me put them deep down under the cloud of forgetting!"

This strikes me as being a very good question. And so I must
reflect in order to answer it as well as my feebleness permits. First,
when you ask me what this thought is that presses so hard upon you
in this exercise, offering to help you in this work, I answer that it is a
well-defined and clear sight of your natural intelligence imprinted

upon your reason within your soul. And when you ask me whether it is good or evil, I say that it must of necessity be always good in its nature, because it is a ray of God's likeness. But the use of it can be both good and evil. It is good when it is illumined by grace, so that you may see your wretched state, the Passion, the kindness and the wonderful works of God in his creatures, bodily and spiritual. And so it is no wonder that it increases your devotion as much as you say. But the use of it is evil when it is swollen with pride and with the curiosity which comes from the subtle speculation and learning, such as theologians have, which makes them want to be known not as humble clerics and masters of divinity or of devotion, but proud scholars of the devil and masters of vanity and falsehood. And in other men and women, whether they be religious or seculars, the use and exercise of this natural understanding is evil when it is swollen with proud and clever learning of worldly things and earthly ideas for the coveting of worldly honors and rich possessions and the pleasure and vainglory which comes from men's flatterings.

Next, you ask me why you should put down such thoughts under the cloud of forgetting, since it is true that they are good of their kind and, when well used, they do you so much good and greatly increase your devotion. My answer is that you must clearly understand that there are two kinds of lives in the holy church. One is the active life, and the other is the contemplative life. The active life is the lower, and the contemplative life is the higher. Active life has two degrees, a higher and a lower; and the contemplative life also has two degrees, a lower and a higher. Further, these two lives are so joined together that, though in part they are different, neither of them can be lived fully without having some part in the other. For the higher part of the active life is the same as the lower part of the contemplative life. Hence, a man cannot be fully active unless he is partly a contemplative, nor can he be fully contemplative here below unless he is in some way active. It is the nature of the active life both to be begun and ended in this life. Not so, however, of the contemplative life, which is begun in this life and shall last without end. That is why the part that Mary chose shall never be taken away [Luke 10:42]. The active life is troubled and anxious about many things; but the contemplative sits in peace, intent only on one thing.

The lower part of the active life consists in good and honest corporal works of mercy and of charity. The higher part of the active life, and the lower part of the contemplative, consists in good spiritual meditations and earnest consideration of a man's own wretched state with sorrow and contrition, of the Passion of Christ and of his servants with pity and compassion, and of the wonderful gifts, kindness, and works of God in all his creatures, corporeal and spiritual, with thanksgiving and praise. But the higher part of contemplation, insofar as it is possible to possess it here below, consists entirely in this darkness and in this cloud of unknowing, with a loving impulse and a dark gazing into the simple being of God himself alone.

In the lower part of the active life, a man is outside himself and beneath himself. In the higher part of the active life, and the lower part of the contemplative life, a man is within himself and on a par with himself. But in the higher part of the contemplative life, a man is above himself and under his God. He is above himself because he makes it his purpose to arrive by grace whither he cannot come by nature, that is to say, to be knit to God in spirit, in oneness of love and union of wills.

One can understand that it is impossible for a man to come to the higher part of the active life unless he leaves, for a time, the lower part. In the same way, a man cannot come to the higher part of the contemplative life unless he leaves for a time the lower part. It would be a wrong thing for a man engaged in meditation, and a hindrance to him, to turn his mind to the outward corporal works which he had done or should do, even though in themselves they are very holy works. In the same way, it would be very inappropriate and a great hindrance to a man who ought to be working in this darkness and in this cloud of unknowing, with an affective impulse of love to God for himself alone, to permit any thought or any meditation on God's wonderful gifts, kindness, or his work in any of his creatures, bodily or spiritual, to rise up in his mind so as to press between him and his God, even if they should be very holy thoughts and give him great happiness and consolation.

This is the reason why I bid you put down any such clear and insinuating thought and cover it up with a thick cloud of forgetting, no matter how holy it might be, and no matter how well it might promise to help you in your endeavor. Because it is love alone that can reach God in this life, and not knowing. For as long as the soul dwells in this mortal body, the clarity of our understanding in the contemplation of all spiritual things, and especially of God, is always mixed up with some sort of imagination; and because of it this exercise of ours would be tainted, and it would be very surprising if it did not lead us into great error.

Chapter 9

During this exercise, the calling to mind
of the holiest creature God ever made is
a hindrance rather than a help.

The intense activity, therefore, of your understanding, which will always press upon you when you set yourself to this dark contemplation, must always be put down. For if you do not put it down, it will put you down; so much so that when you imagine that you can best abide in this darkness and that nothing is in your mind except God alone, if you take a close look, you will find that your mind is occupied not with this darkness, but with a clear picture of something beneath God. If this is in fact so, then indeed that thing is above you for the moment and between you and your God. So set yourself to put down such clear pictures, no matter how holy or how pleasant they may be.

One thing I must tell you. This blind impulse of love toward God for himself alone, this secret love beating on this cloud of unknowing, is more profitable for the salvation of your soul, more worthy in itself, and more pleasing to God and to all the saints and angels in heaven; yes, and of more use to all your friends both bodily and spiritually, whether they are alive or dead. And it is better for you to experience this spiritually in your affection than it is to have the eye of your soul opened in contemplation either in seeing all the angels and the saints in heaven or in hearing all the mirth or the melody that is among those who are in bliss.

Nor need you be surprised at what I say, for if you could once see it as clearly as you can come by grace to touch it and to experience it in this life, you would think as I do. But take it for granted that no man shall ever have such clear sight here in this life; but the feeling—that a man can have through grace, when God deigns to grant it. So lift up your love to that cloud or, rather, if I am to speak more truthfully, let God draw your love up to that cloud, and try, through the help of his grace, to forget every other thing.

A simple awareness of anything under God which forces itself upon your will and consciousness puts you farther away from God than you would be if it did not exist; it hinders you and makes you less able to feel, by experience, the fruit of his love. How much more, then, do you think that an awareness which is drawn to yourself knowingly and deliberately will hinder you in your purpose? And if the consciousness of any particular saint or pure spiritual thing hinders you so much, how much more do you think that the consciousness of any living person in this wretched life or any corporal or worldly thing will hinder you and be an obstacle to you in this exercise?

I am not saying that any such simple, sudden thought of any good and pure spiritual thing under God which presses against your will or your understanding, or is willfully drawn into your mind deliberately in order to increase your devotion, is therefore evil, even though it is a hindrance to this sort of exercise; and God forbid that you should understand it so! But I do say that, in spite of its goodness and holiness, in this exercise it is more of a hindrance than a help—I mean during the time of the exercise. For certainly, he who seeks to have God perfectly will not take his rest in the consciousness of any angel or any saint that is in heaven.

Chapter 10

How to know when a thought is not
sinful, and when a sinful thought is
capital or venial.

But if any living person, man or woman, comes to mind, or any
bodily or worldly thing whatever, the case is quite different. A
simple thought of any of these which comes up against your will
and your consciousness, though it is not a sin imputed to you, is
the effect, beyond your control, of original sin from which you
were cleansed in your baptism. Nonetheless, if this sudden
impulse or thought is not beaten down straightaway, your fleshly
heart, because of its frailty, will be immediately affected with
some kind of pleasure if the thing pleases you or has pleased you
before, or with some kind of resentment if it is a thing which
you imagine upsets you or has upset you before.

Such a sinful affection can be grave in worldly men and
women who have been living in serious sin. But the same affection which causes pleasure or resentment in the fleshly heart is
no more than venial sin in you and in all others who have, with a
sincere will, forsaken the world and have bound themselves in
any way, privately or openly, to the devout life in the holy church,
and who therefore wish to be governed not according to their
own will and understanding, but according to the will and the
counsel of their superiors, whoever they are, religious or secular.
This is because your intention has been rooted and grounded in

God from the time when you first began to live according to the state of life in which you now persevere. But if it should happen that this affection which causes pleasure or resentment in your fleshly heart be allowed to remain there for any length of time without being repudiated, it will eventually become fastened to the spiritual heart (that is to say, the will) with full consent; then it will be deadly sin.

This happens when you, or any of those of whom I am speaking, willfully bring up in their mind any living person, man or woman, or any bodily or worldly thing whatsoever. To the extent that it is a thing which grieves or has grieved you before, there rises up in you a spiteful passion and an appetite for vengeance; then it is called wrath. Or else there rises up a fierce contempt and some kind of loathing for a person along with spiteful and disapproving thoughts; this is called envy. Or else a weariness and a repugnance for any good occupation, bodily or spiritual; this is called sloth. If it is a thing that pleases you or has pleased you before, there rises up in you a keen delight in thinking about it, whatever it is, so much so that you take your rest in that thought, and finally fasten your heart and will to it, and feed your carnal love upon it. During that time you think that you covet no other wealth except always to live in this peace and rest with the thing that you are thinking about. If this thought, which you bring to mind yourself in this way or else take to yourself when it is brought to your mind and rest in it thus with delight, concerns natural or intellectual talents, or worthiness of favor or of rank, or of comeliness or beauty, then it is pride. If it is a thought of any sort of worldly possessions, riches or cattle, or whatever man can possess or be master of, then it is covetousness. If it concerns delicacies in food or drink or any sort of pleasure which comes from the sense of taste, then it is gluttony. If it concerns the pleasures of love or any kind of fleshly dalliance, for the seduction or flattery of any living person, man or woman, then it is called lust.

Chapter 11

Each thought and impulse is to be given
its proper value; carelessness in venial
sin is always to be avoided.

I do not say this because you, or any of the others I have mentioned, are guilty and burdened with any such sins, but because I
want you to reckon each thought and each impulse at its proper
value and to work earnestly to destroy the first impulse and
thought of those things in which you can thus commit sin. For
there is one thing I must tell you: he who takes no account of or
pays little heed to the first thought, even though there is no sin
in it for him, whoever he may be, cannot avoid carelessness with
regard to venial sin. No one can keep absolutely clear of venial
sin in this mortal life [cf. 1 John 1:8]. However, carelessness in
venial sin should always be avoided by all true disciples of perfection [cf. Matt. 19:21]. Otherwise I would not be surprised if
they soon commit grievous sin.

Chapter 12

By means of this exercise sin is destroyed
and virtues are acquired.

If, then, you are determined to stand and not to fall [cf. 1 Cor. 10:12], never cease from your endeavor, but constantly beat with a sharp dart of longing love upon this cloud of unknowing which is between you and your God. Avoid thinking of anything under God, and do not leave this exercise no matter what happens. For it alone, of itself, destroys the root and the ground of sin [cf. Rom. 6:6]. No matter how much you fast or keep watch, no matter how early you rise, no matter how hard your bed, no matter how rough your hair shirt; yes, and if it were lawful to do so, as it is not, even were you to put out your eyes, cut out your tongue from your mouth, stop up your ears and nose, though you were to cut away your private parts [cf. Matt. 19:12] and cause your body all the pain that you could think of; all this would be of no avail at all to you. The impulse and tendency to sin would still be in you.

Yes, and more than this. No matter how much you were to weep and sorrow for your sins, or for the Passion of Christ, or be ever so mindful of the joys of heaven, what would it profit you [cf. 1 Cor. 13:3]? Certainly it would be of great good, great help, great gain, and great grace. But in comparison with that blind impulse of love, there is little it can or may do. This, without all those other things, is Mary's best part. Without it they profit little or nothing. Not only does it destroy the root and ground of sin, as far as that is possible here below, but it also acquires the virtues. For when it is truly implanted, all the virtues will be perfectly and delicately implanted, experienced, and contained in it, without any mixture of motive. And no matter how many virtues a man may have, without this they will all be mixed with some crooked motive, and therefore they will be imperfect.

For virtue is nothing else than an ordered and controlled affection which has God for its single object, himself alone. For he himself is the pure cause of all the virtues; so much so that if a man is moved to any virtue by any other cause besides God, even though he is the chief cause, that virtue will be imperfect. An example of this may be seen in one or two virtues which can stand for all the others. The two virtues meekness and charity are good examples, for whoever can have these two would clearly need no others; he would have them all.

Chapter 13

The nature of humility; perfect and
imperfect humility.

Let us look first at the virtue of humility. See how it is imperfect
when it flows from any other source which mingles with the
chief, though this be God, and how it is perfect when its single
source is God himself. First, if the matter is to be truly appre-
hended and understood, we must know what humility is in
itself. Then we shall be able to understand more clearly in truth
of spirit what its cause is.

In itself, humility is nothing else but a man's true understanding
and awareness of himself as he really is. It is certain that if a man
could truly see and be conscious of himself as he really is, he would
indeed be truly humble. There are two causes of this meekness. One
is the foulness, wretchedness, and weakness into which a man has
fallen by sin. As long as he lives in this life, no matter how holy he
is, he must always experience this in some measure. The other is the
superabundant love and worthiness of God himself. At the sight of
this, all nature trembles, all learned men are fools, and all the saints
and angels are blinded; so much so that were it not for the wisdom
of his Godhead, whereby due proportion is set between their contemplation and their natural and grace-given capacity, I would be at
a loss to say what would happen to them.

This second cause of humility is perfect, because it will last
forever. The first cause is imperfect: not only because it is to pass

away at the end of this life, but also because it can often happen, through the abundance of the grace which increases its desire as often and for as long as God deigns to grant it, that a soul living in this mortal flesh may suddenly lose and forget all awareness and experience of its own being, so that it takes no account of its holiness or its wretchedness. But whether this experience happens often or seldom to a soul so disposed by God, my belief is that the experience lasts only a very short while. During this time it is made perfectly humble, for it has neither knowledge nor experience of any cause but the chief one. But whenever it has knowledge and experience of the other, along with the chief cause, then its humility is imperfect. It is, however, good, and we must always have it; and God forbid that you should understand it in any other way than I say.

Chapter 14

In this life it is impossible for a sinner
to reach the perfection of humility
unless imperfect humility comes first.

I would rather have this true knowledge and experience of myself as the wretch that I am, even though I call it imperfect humility, because I believe that it would quickly obtain for me the perfect cause and virtue of humility; sooner, indeed, than if all the saints and angels in heaven and all men and women who are living on earth in the holy church, religious or secular, in every degree of life were all of them together to do nothing else but pray to God for me to obtain this perfect humility. Yes, indeed. It is impossible for a sinner to obtain the perfect virtue of humility, or to keep it when it is acquired, without the imperfect humility.

So labor and toil as much as you can and know how to acquire for yourself the true knowledge and experience of yourself as the wretch that you are. And then I think that, soon after, you will have a true knowledge and experience of God as he is—not as he is in himself, for no one can experience that except God himself [cf. John 1:18], nor as you shall experience him in blessedness, both body and soul together—but inasmuch as this is possible and as it is his good pleasure to be known and experienced by a humble soul living in this mortal body [cf. Matt. 11:27–30].

Nor must you think, because I set down two causes of humility, one perfect and the other imperfect, that I wish you to leave off striving for imperfect humility and concentrate entirely on acquiring the perfect. Indeed, I do not believe that you could ever so acquire it. But I write as I do with the intention of letting you know and showing you the worthiness of this spiritual exercise above every other bodily or spiritual exercise which man can or may perform by grace: how that hidden love, raised up in purity of spirit upon this dark cloud of unknowing between you and your God, delicately and perfectly contains in itself the perfect virtue of humility, without any particular or clearly defined sight of anything under God. And also I wish you to know what perfect humility is and set it as a sign upon the love of your heart [cf. Song of Sol. 8:6], and do so both for you and for me, since it is my wish, by this knowledge, to make you more humble. For it often happens that a lack of knowledge is the cause of great pride, or so it seems to me.

Again, it might be that if you did not know what perfect meekness is, you might think, because you had a little knowledge and experience of what I call imperfect humility, that you had almost reached perfect humility. So you would deceive yourself, thinking that you were very humble, when in fact you were wrapped around in foul-stinking pride. So set yourself to labor for perfect humility, because its nature is such that if a man has it, and as long as he has it, he will not sin, and afterwards only a little.

Chapter 15

A brief refutation of the error which
maintains that there is no better means
of humbling oneself than by calling to
mind one's own sinfulness.

Have a steadfast trust that there is the sort of perfect humility mentioned above, and that through grace it can be acquired in this life. I say this to refute the error of those who declare that there is no more perfect cause of humility than that which springs from the awareness of our wretchedness and of our past sins.

I readily grant that for those who sin habitually, as I do myself and have done, here is the most necessary and expedient cause: to be humbled under the awareness of our wretchedness and of our past sins until such time as the complete rust of our sins is for the most part scrubbed away, according to the witness of our conscience and our spiritual director.

But to others who are to all intents and purposes innocent, who have never sinned seriously with determined will and awareness, but only through frailty and ignorance, and who set themselves to be contemplatives, and to both of us as well: if our spiritual director and our conscience alike bear witness to our proper amendment in contrition and confession and satisfaction according to the law and ordinance of the holy church, and as long as we are aware that we are moved and called by grace to be contemplatives—there is then another cause for being humbled.

This is as far above the first as is the life of our Lady, St. Mary, above that of the most sinful penitent in the holy church, or as the life of Christ is above that of any other man in this life, or as that of an angel in heaven who never experienced weakness, nor ever shall, is above the life of the frailest man here in this world.

For if there were no more perfect cause of humility than to see and experience one's wretchedness, I would like to ask those who allege this to be true, under what cause were they humbled who never saw or experienced wretchedness or stirring of sin, nor ever shall, as it is of our Lord, Jesus Christ, our Lady, St. Mary, and all the saints and angels in heaven? It is to this and to every kind of perfection that our Lord Jesus Christ himself calls us in the gospel, where he tells us that we are to be as perfect by grace as he himself is by nature [Matt. 5:48].

Chapter 16

> By means of this exercise, the sinner
> who is truly converted and called to
> contemplation reaches perfection more
> quickly than by any other exercise and
> obtains from God a most speedy for-
> giveness of his sins.

No man should think it presumptuous, because he is the most wretched sinner alive, to dare take upon himself—after he has made lawful amendment and has felt himself called to the life that is termed contemplative with the agreement of his spiritual director and in accord with his own conscience—to offer a humble impulse of love to his God, knocking secretly on the cloud of unknowing between him and his God. Our Lord said to Mary, who stands for all sinners called to the contemplative life: "Your sins are forgiven you" [Luke 7:47–48]. This was not because of her great sorrow, or her awareness of her sins, or the humility that she had at the sight of her wretchedness. It was because, surely, that she loved much. Here, then, can men see what this hidden impulse of love can win from our Lord, over and above every other exercise that a man may think to perform.

Yet I readily agree that she had great sorrow, wept very bitterly for her sins [Luke 7:37–38], and that she was greatly humbled by the awareness of her wretchedness. We should do likewise, who have been wretches and habitual sinners all our life long;

our sorrow for our sins should indeed be exceedingly great, and we should be deeply humbled in the awareness of our wretchedness [cf. Ps. 51:9; Luke 15:18].

How? Surely, just as Mary did. For although she could never rid herself of the deep sorrow of her heart for her sins, all her lifetime she carried them with her wherever she went, as it were in a bundle bound together and stored secretly in the cavern of her heart, in a way that could never be forgotten. Yet it still can be said, and is affirmed by holy Scripture, that she had a greater sorrow of heart for her lack of love than for any awareness of her sins. She had a more sorrowing desire, a deeper sighing; she languished almost to the point of death for her lack of love, though she had very great love. And we are not to wonder at this, for it is the nature of a true lover that the more he loves, the more he longs to love.

Yet she knew well, by her own experience in sober truth, that she was a viler wretch than anyone else and that her sins had made a division between her and her God, whom she loved so much; and also that they were in great part the cause of this lingering sickness through lacking of love. What then did she do? Did she for this reason come down from the heights of her desire to the depths of her sinful life and search about in the foul, malodorous bog and dunghill of her sins, dragging them up one by one with all their circumstances and sorrowing and weeping upon each one of them? No, indeed, she did nothing of the sort. And why? Because God made her understand, by the grace within her soul, that she would never achieve anything thus. She was more likely by these means to raise up in herself a tendency to sin again, rather than to obtain by such methods a true forgiveness of all her sins.

So she hung up her love and her longing desire in this cloud of unknowing, and learned to love what she could not see clearly in this life by the light of understanding in her reason or yet truly experience in sweetness of love in her affection; so much so that often enough she paid but little attention to whether she had been a sinner or not. Yes, indeed; I expect that very often she was so deeply moved in her affection by the love of his Godhead that she had no eyes for the beauty of his precious and blessed body as he sat in his loveliness, speaking and preaching to her; nor of anything else, corporal or spiritual [cf. Luke 10:39–42]. That this is true, the gospel appears to be witness.

Chapter 17

The true contemplative has no desire to concern himself with the active life or with what is done or spoken against him; he must not try to explain himself to his detractors.

In the gospel of St. Luke it is written that when our Lord was in the house of Martha, all the time that Martha was busying herself with the preparation of his food, her sister Mary sat at his feet [Luke 10:38–42]. In listening to him, she had no time for the busy activity of her sister, even though this activity was very good and holy, for it is the first part of the active life. Nor was she paying attention to the preciousness of his blessed body or to the sweet voice and words of his manhood, though this is better and holier, for it is the second part of the active life and the first of the contemplative life. She was contemplating, with all the love of her heart, the supreme and sovereign wisdom of his Godhead clothed in the dark words of his manhood. She had no desire to leave off, not for anything she saw or heard spoken going on around her. But she sat unmoving, sending up many a sweet and longing impulse of love to beat upon that high cloud of unknowing between her and her God.

For one thing I must tell you. There never yet existed, nor ever shall, so pure a creature, one so ravished on high in contemplation and love of the Godhead, who did not find this high and wonderful cloud of unknowing between him and his God. It was in this cloud that Mary was occupied, sending forth her hidden impulses of love. Why? This is the best and holiest part of contemplation that may be had in this life, and it was her desire never to leave this part for anything; so much so that when her sister Martha complained about her to our Lord and bade him command her sister to get up and help her and not to leave her to work and labor by herself, Mary sat in silence and answered not a word. She did not offer so much as a frown toward her sister for any complaint that she could make. And no wonder: because she had another work to do of which Martha knew nothing. Therefore she had no leisure to listen to her or to answer her complaints.

You see, my friend, all these works, words, and looks that passed between our Lord and these two sisters are given as an example of all actives and all contemplatives that have lived in the holy church since that time, and shall live, until the day of judgment. For Mary stands for all contemplatives, who should conform their behavior to hers; and in the same way Martha stands for the actives, according to the same comparison.

Chapter 18

Actives still complain about contemplatives, as Martha complained of Mary; the
cause of these complaints is ignorance.

Just as Martha complained about her sister Mary, in the same
way, even to this day, all actives complain about contemplatives.
Whenever a man or a woman living in any company in this
world—whether it be religious or secular, it makes no differ-
ence—is aware that he is being moved through grace and with
the advice of his director to forsake all outward business and set
himself entirely to live the contemplative life, as best he knows
how and according as his conscience and his spiritual director
advise him, then straightway his brothers and sisters, all his best
friends, and many others who are ignorant of his inward movements and of that manner of life which he sets himself to live
turn upon him with many complaints. They reprove him sharply,
saying that what he is doing is nothing. And they begin to tell
him stories, true as well as fictitious, of men and women who
have fallen away after giving themselves to the contemplative life.
But they never say anything about those who persevere.

I agree that there are many who appear to have forsaken the
world who do fall away and have fallen away in the past and,
instead of becoming God's servants and his contemplatives, have
become the devil's, because they would not permit themselves to
be governed by true spiritual counsel. And so they turn out to be

hypocrites or heretics, or they fall into frenzies and many other kinds of misfortune, to the scandal of the all-holy church. But I shall say no more of them at this time, lest we digress. Later on perhaps, God willing and if need be, we may say something about the nature and causes of their falling away. Let us leave them for the moment and get on with our subject.

Chapter 19

A brief apology by the author of this
book; all contemplatives must wholly
excuse all actives for their complaints of
word or deed.

Some may think that I do little honor to Martha, that special
saint, because I draw a parallel between her complaints against
her sister with worldly men's words, or theirs with hers. But
truly I do not mean any dishonor to her or to them. God forbid
that in this book I should say anything that might be taken as a
rebuke to any of the servants of God in any degree, particularly
of his special saint. For I believe that every excuse should be
made for her complaining, if we take into account the time and
the way in which she spoke. Her ignorance was the cause of
what she said. It is no wonder that she did not know, at that
time, how Mary was occupied, for I believe that up to then she
had heard but little of this perfection. Also, what she said was
said courteously and in a few words; therefore there is every
excuse for her.

Similarly, it seems to me that men and women living the active
life in the world should also have every excuse made for them
when they complain in the manner we have mentioned before,
even though what they say is said rudely, for we must make
allowance for their ignorance. Just as Martha had very little knowledge of what her sister Mary was doing when she complained of

her to our Lord, in the same way these people nowadays have little or no knowledge of what these young disciples of God are about when they turn from the business of this world and dispose themselves to be God's special servants in holiness and righteousness of spirit. If they did know, I daresay that they would neither do nor say as they do. So it seems to me that we must always make every excuse for them, because they know no better way of life than that which they live themselves. Furthermore, when I reflect on my own innumerable faults which I have committed myself in time past, both by word and deed, because of my ignorance, it seems to me that, if I myself would have God excuse me for faults I have committed in ignorance, then I should in charity and compassion always excuse the ignorant words and deeds of other men. Otherwise I am not doing to others as I would that others did to me [Matt. 7:12].

Chapter 20

Almighty God will answer well enough
for those who have no desire to leave
their occupation of loving him in order
to make excuses for themselves.

So it seems to me that they who are set on being contemplatives should not only make excuses for active men who complain about them, but it seems to me also that they should be so occupied in spirit that they take little or no heed of what men might do or say concerning them. That was what Mary did, who is an example for us all, when her sister Martha complained to our Lord. And if we do that sincerely, our Lord will do now for us what he did then for Mary.

What was that? It was this. Our loving Lord Jesus Christ, to whom nothing is secret, though Martha asked him to act as judge and to bid Mary rise up and help her to serve him, yet because he saw that Mary was fervently occupied in spirit with the love of his Godhead, he answered courteously and reasonably, as became him, on behalf of her who would not leave his love in order to excuse herself. And how did he answer? Indeed, not merely as a judge to whom Martha had appealed, but as an advocate he lawfully defended her who loved him. And he said, "Martha, Martha." In his urgency he called her name twice, because he wanted her to hear him and to take heed of his words. "You are much occupied," he said, "and troubled about many things." For they who are actives must always be occupied and busy about many different things, which are given to them first for their own use, and then for acts of mercy toward their fellow Christians, as charity demands. This our Lord said to Martha because he wished to let her know that her business was good and profitable for her soul's salvation. But lest she should think that this is the best work that a person might do, he added these words: "Only one thing is necessary" [Luke 10:42].

What is that one thing? Surely that God may be loved and praised for himself above all other business, bodily or spiritual, that man can do. And lest Martha might think that she could both love and praise God above all other business, bodily or spiritual, and at the same time be busy about the necessities of this life, he wished to make it clear to her that she could not serve God both in corporal works and in spiritual works together perfectly (imperfectly she could, but not perfectly). So he added to what he had said that Mary had chosen the best part, which would never be taken away from her. Because that perfect movement of love which is begun here is equal in all respects with what shall last without end in the bliss of heaven; they are both one.

Chapter 21

The correct interpretation of the gospel
text "Mary has chosen the best part."

What is the meaning of "Mary has chosen the best"? Wherever
the best is declared or named, it demands that two things should
precede it, a good and a better, in order that itself may be the
best, the third in number. What are these three good things, of
which Mary chose the best? Three lives they are not, for the holy
church only takes account of two, the active life and the contemplative life. These two lives are allegorically understood in this
gospel story of these two sisters, Martha and Mary: by Martha,
the active; by Mary, the contemplative. Outside of these two
lives, no man can be saved; and where there are no more than
two, no man can choose the best.

But though there are only two lives, yet in these two there are
three parts, each one better than the other. And these three have
been set out specifically in their places earlier on in this book.
For, as we have said, the first part consists in good and honest corporal works of mercy and charity. This is the first degree of the
active life, as was noted above. The second part of these two lives
consists in good spiritual meditations on a man's own wretchedness, on the Passion of Christ, and the joys of heaven. The first
part is good, but this part is better, for this is the second degree of
the active life and the first of the contemplative life. In this part
the contemplative life and the active life are joined together in

spiritual relationship. They are made sisters after the example of Martha and Mary. An active may make progress in contemplation thus far and no farther, unless very seldom and by a special grace. A contemplative may not descend any lower toward active life than this, except very seldom and when there is great need.

The third part of these two lives stands in this dark cloud of unknowing, with many secret impulses of love toward God himself. The first part is good, the second is better, but the third is the best of all. This is Mary's best part; and therefore it is clearly to be understood that our Lord did not say, "Mary has chosen the best life," for there are only two lives, and of two no man can choose the best. But of these two lives, "Mary has chosen," he said, "the best part, which shall never be taken away from her." The first part and the second, although both are good and holy, yet they end with this life. For in the other life, it will not be necessary to exercise ourselves in the works of mercy or to weep for our wretchedness or for the Passion of Christ. For then no one shall be hungry or thirsty, no one shall die for cold, or be sick or without lodging or in prison or need burial [cf. Matt. 25:35–36], for then no one shall die anymore [Rev. 21:4]. But the third part, which Mary chose, let those choose who are called to it by grace; or to speak more truly, let those who are chosen for it by God tend toward it with desire. For that shall never be taken away; if it begin here, it will last without end.

So let the voice of our Lord cry to these actives as if he were speaking now to them on our behalf, as he did then for Mary to Martha. "Martha, Martha": "Actives, actives, busy you now as best you can in the first part and in the second, now in the one and now in the other; and if you so desire and feel yourselves so disposed, in both at once. But do not meddle with contemplatives; you do not know what they are about. Let them sit at their rest and at their play, with the third and the best part of Mary."

Chapter 22

The wonderful love of Christ for Mary, who represents all sinners truly converted and called to the grace of contemplation.

Sweet was that love between our Lord and Mary. She had great love for him, but his for her was greater. And if a man would contemplate aright all the looks that passed between him and her not according to the words of a gossip, but according to the witness of the gospel story which cannot in any way be false, he will find that her heart was so set on loving him that nothing beneath him could bring her comfort or keep her heart from him. This is she, that same Mary, who, when she sought him at the sepulcher with tears running down her face, refused to be comforted by angels [cf. Matt. 28:1–2; John 20:11–12]. For when they spoke to her with such sweetness and such love and said: "Do not weep, Mary, because our Lord whom you seek is risen, and you shall possess him, and see him alive in all his beauty among his disciples in Galilee, as he said" [Matt. 28:5–7], she would not go away on that account, because it seemed to her that when people truly seek the king of angels, they ought not to leave off because of angels.

Furthermore, whoever will examine carefully the gospel story will find many wonderful examples of perfect love written about her for our instruction which are also in accord with the exercise described in this book, as though they had been set down and written for this very purpose. And, indeed, so they were, if anyone can rightly understand them.

If anyone wants to see in the gospel account the wonderful and special love that our Lord had for Mary, who stands for all habitual sinners truly converted and called to the grace of contemplation, he will find that our Lord could not allow any man or woman, not even her own sister, to speak a word against her without himself answering for her. Furthermore, he reproached Simon the leper in his own house, because his thoughts were against her [cf. Luke 7:40; Mark 14:3]. This was great love; this was surpassing love.

Chapter 23

It is God's will spiritually to provide and
answer for those who have no desire to
provide and answer for themselves,
because of their preoccupation with his
love.

Truly, then, if we are ready to conform our love and our living,
insofar as is possible for us by grace and by direction, to the love
and the living of Mary, there is no doubt that he shall answer
now for us spiritually in the same way, every day, in the hearts of
all those that either speak or think against us. And not but what
there will always be someone to think or speak something
against us as long as we live this life of travail, even as they did
against Mary [cf. Matt. 5:11–12]. But I say that if we pay no more
heed to what they say or think, and do not give up this hidden
ghostly work because of their words or their thoughts, any more
than she did, our Lord, I say, will answer them in spirit, as long
as all is well with them who so think and speak, to such effect
that within a few days they will be ashamed of their words and
their thoughts [cf. Ps. 6:10].

Just as he will answer for us in this way in spirit, so he will
direct other men in spirit to provide us with all that is necessary
for this life, such as food and clothes and everything else, when
he sees that we refuse to leave off the work of his love to busy
ourselves about those things. I say this in refutation of the error of

those who maintain that it is not lawful for men to devote themselves to the service of God in the contemplative life unless they
are assured beforehand of having what is necessary for the body
[cf. Matt. 6:31–33]. For they say that God sends the cow, but not
by the horn. Now they are wrong to say this of God, as they well
know. For if you, whoever you are, have been sincerely converted
from the world to God, you must trust steadfastly that God will
give you, without your attending to it, one of two things: either
an abundance of what is necessary or strength in body and spiritual patience [cf. Gal. 5:22] to put up with the lack of them. What
then does it matter which of these two a man has? For true contemplatives it is all the same. And whoever is doubtful of this,
either the devil is in his heart and robs him of his faith, or else he
is not yet as truly converted to God as he should be, no matter
how clever or holy the reasons which he puts up against it, whoever he may be.

So you who set yourself to be a contemplative as Mary was,
choose rather to be humbled under the wonderful height and
worthiness of God [1 Pet. 5:6], which is perfect, rather than
under your own wretchedness, which is imperfect. That is to say,
take care that you make the worthiness of God the object of your
special contemplation, rather than your own wretchedness. For
they who are perfectly humble shall never lack anything, corporal
or spiritual. The reason is that they have God, in whom is all
abundance; whoever has him, indeed, as this book says, needs
nothing else in this life.

Chapter 24

The nature of charity; it is subtly and perfectly contained in the exercise described
in this book.

We have said that humility is subtly and perfectly contained in this
little blind impulse of love as it beats upon this dark cloud of
unknowing, with all other things put down and forgotten. The
same is to be understood of all the other virtues, and particularly
of charity. We are to understand that charity means nothing else
than loving God for himself above all creatures, and loving man
equal to the love of yourself for God's sake [cf. Luke 10:27; Deut.
6:5; Lev. 19:18]. It is very obvious that in this exercise God is
loved for himself above all creatures. For, as was said before, the
essence of this exercise is nothing else but a simple and direct
reaching out to God for himself. I call it a simple reaching out,
because in this exercise the perfect apprentice does not ask to be
released from pain or for his reward to be increased; in a word,
he asks for nothing but God himself, so much so that he takes no
account or regard of whether he is in pain or in joy, but only that
the will of him whom he loves be fulfilled. It is evident, then, that
in this exercise God is perfectly loved for himself, and above all
creatures. In this exercise, the perfect worker will not permit his
awareness of the holiest creature God ever made to have any share.

Experience shows that in this exercise, the second, the lower
branch of charity, that for your fellow Christian, is truly and

perfectly fulfilled. For the perfect worker here has no special regard for any individual, whether he is kinsman or stranger, friend or foe. For he considers all men alike as his kinsmen and no man a stranger to him. He considers all men his friends and none his foes. So much so that he considers all those that cause him pain and do him mischief in this life to be his very special friends, and he considers that he is being moved to wish them as much good as he would to the dearest friend he has [cf. Matt. 5:44–48].

Chapter 25

During the time of this exercise, the
perfect soul has no special regard for
any particular person in this life.

During this exercise, I say that he must not have any special
regard for anyone alive, whether friend or foe, kinsman or
stranger. For if this exercise is to be done perfectly, that cannot
be, as so it is when all things under God are entirely forgotten,
which is fitting for this exercise. But I avow that he shall be made
so virtuous and so charitable by reason of this exercise that,
when he comes down to frequent the company of or to pray for
his fellow Christians, his will shall be directed as particularly
toward his foe as toward his friend, toward the stranger as
toward his kinsman. I do not mean that he comes down from
this work completely, for that cannot be without great sin, but
rather from the height of the contemplative exercise, which he
must do sometimes when it is expedient and necessary according
to the demands of charity. Yes, and sometimes his will must be
directed rather to his foe than to his friend [cf. Luke 6:27–36].

It must be said, however, that in this exercise he has not the leisure
to consider who is his friend or foe, kinsman or stranger. I am not saying that he is not to feel sometimes, and even often, that in his affection he is more drawn to one or two or three than to all the rest; that
is lawful for many reasons, and as charity demands. Such special affection Christ our Lord had for John and Mary and Peter before many

others [cf. John 13:23; 19:26; 20:2; 21:15–17]. What I say is that in the time of this exercise all alike should be dear to him, because then he will experience no cause for affection except God alone. Thus, all will be loved plainly and simply for God, and in the same degree as he loves himself.

For as all men were lost in Adam [cf. Rom. 5:12–21], and as all men who bear witness to their desire of salvation by good works are saved and shall be by the power of Christ's Passion alone, a soul whose affection is perfectly extended in this exercise and thus united to God in spirit, not exactly in the same way, but as it were in the same way, does all that in it lies, as the experience of this exercise bears witness, to make all men as perfect in this work as it is itself. For just as when a limb of our body feels sore, all the other limbs are in pain and ill-affected on that account [cf. 1 Cor. 12:12, 22], or when one limb is in good health, all the rest are likewise in good health; so it is, spiritually, with all the limbs of the holy church. For Christ is our Head and we are the limbs, as long as we are in charity [cf. Eph. 5:23]. And whoever desires to be a perfect disciple of our Lord is called upon to lift up his spirit in this spiritual exercise for the salvation of all his natural brothers and sisters, as our Lord lifted up his body on the cross. And how? Not for his friends and his kinsfolk and for those who love him dearly, but in general, for all mankind, without any special regard for one more than for another. For all those who desire to forsake sin and ask for mercy are to be saved through the power of his Passion.

What has been said of humility and charity is to be understood of all the other virtues, for they are all subtly contained in this little impulse of love mentioned before.

Chapter 26

This exercise is extremely laborious except with very special graces or habitual cooperation with ordinary graces over a long period; the distinction in this exercise between the activity of the soul supported by grace and the activity of God alone.

So now labor earnestly for a short while and beat upon this high cloud of unknowing, and then take your rest. For whoever is to become accustomed to this exercise will have hard labor; yes, and very hard labor indeed, unless he receive a very special grace, or else it has become a habit with him over a long period.

But, you may ask, in what does this labor consist? Surely not in that devout impulse of love that is continually worked in the will not by the soul itself, but by the hand of almighty God, which is always ready to perform this work in every soul that is disposed for it and does all that it can, and has done for a long time, to make itself ready for this exercise? And so, you may ask, where precisely is the labor? The work consists in the treading down of the awareness of all the creatures that God ever made and in keeping them under the cloud of forgetting, as we mentioned before. Here is all the labor; for this, with the help of grace, is man's work. And the other beyond this, the impulse of love, this is the work of God alone. So press on with your own work, and he, I promise you, will certainly not fail in his.

Press on then earnestly, and show your mettle. Do you not see how he is standing waiting for you? For shame! Labor earnestly for a little while, and you will soon find rest from the severity and the hardship of that work [cf. Matt. 11:28–30]. For though it is hard and constraining in the beginning when you have no devotion, nevertheless afterward, when you have devotion, it shall become very restful and very easy for you, though it was so hard before. Then you shall have very little labor, or none at all. For then God will work sometimes all by himself, although not always or even for a long time together, but when it pleases him and as it pleases him; then it will seem to you a joyful thing to leave him to get on with it.

Then perhaps it will be his will to send out a ray of spiritual light piercing this cloud of unknowing between you and him, and he will show you some of his secrets, of which man may not or cannot speak [cf. 2 Cor. 12:4]. Then you shall feel your affection all aflame with the fire of his love, far more than I know how to tell you or may or wish to at this time. For I dare not take it upon myself to speak with my blabbing, fleshly tongue of the work that belongs to God alone; and, to put it briefly, even though I dared so to speak, I would not wish to. But I am very pleased to speak to you of the work that falls to man, when he feels himself moved and helped by grace; for it is less hazardous to speak of this than of the other.

Chapter 27

Who should undertake this grace-giving
exercise.

First and foremost, I will tell you who should give himself to this
exercise, and when and by what means, and what discretion you
ought to have in it. If you ask me who should give himself to it, I
answer, all who have with a sincere will forsaken the world and
who give themselves not to the active life, but to that life which
is called the contemplative. All these should give themselves to
this grace and to this exercise, whoever they are, whether they
have been habitual sinners or not.

Chapter 28

No one should presume to undertake
this exercise until he has been lawfully
absolved in his conscience of all his particular sins.

If you ask me when they should begin to undertake this exercise,
I answer you and say, not before they have cleansed their conscience of all the particular sins that they have committed beforehand, according to the ordinary direction of the holy church.

In this exercise the whole root and the ground of sin which
always remains in a soul after confession, no matter how earnest it
has been, all withers away. Whoever, then, wishes to undertake this
exercise, let him first purify his conscience; and then when he has
done all that he can in fulfillment of the church's law, let him dispose himself boldly but humbly for this exercise. Let him consider
that he has been kept from it for too long, for this is the exercise in
which a person should labor all his lifetime, even though he may
never have sinned seriously.

As long as a man lives in this mortal flesh, he will always see and
feel this thick cloud of unknowing between himself and God. And
not only that, but it is one of the painful results of original sin that
he will always see and feel that some of the many creatures that God
made, or some of their works, will always be inserting themselves
in his awareness, between himself and God. This is the just judgment of God: that man, when he had the sovereignty and lordship

over all other creatures, willfully made himself subservient to the desires of his subjects, forsaking the commandment of his God and maker [cf. Gen. 2:19; 3:11]. In the same way, now that he wishes to fulfill the commandment of God, he sees and feels that all the creatures that should be beneath him are proudly pressing above him, between himself and his God.

Chapter 29

A man must labor at this exercise perse-
veringly, enduring the pain of it and
judging no one.

Therefore, whoever desires to come to the purity which he lost because of sin, and to arrive at that well-being where all sorrow passes away, must persevere in the labor of this exercise and endure the pain of it, whoever he be, whether he has been a habitual sinner or not.

All men find this exercise laborious, both sinners and those innocents who have never sinned grievously. Those who have been sinners find it much more laborious than those who have not; and that is very reasonable. And yet it often happens that some who have been wicked and habitual sinners come more quickly to the perfection of this exercise than those who have not. This is a mira-cle of mercy from our Lord, who gives his grace in this special way, to the wonder of all the world. But truly, I look forward to the delight of judgment day when God and all his gifts shall be seen clearly. And then some who are now despised and considered as of little or no account, as common sinners, and perhaps some that are now wicked sinners will take their rightful place in his sight with the saints; and some of those who now appear to be very holy and are honored by men for their angelic behavior and some of those who perhaps have never sinned seriously will have their place in sadness among the calves of hell [cf. Ps. 106:19].

From this you must see that no man should be judged by others here in this life, neither for the good nor the evil that they do [cf. Matt. 7:1]. Of course it is lawful to judge whether the deeds are good or evil, but not the men.

Chapter 30

Who should judge or reprehend the
faults of others.

And who, I pray, are to judge the deeds of others? Surely those
who have power over and care of their souls, whether this power
is given externally by the statute and the law of the all-holy
church or else interiorly in spirit by the special impulse of the
Holy Spirit in perfect charity. Every man must take care not to
presume to arrogate to himself the condemnation or reprehen-
sion of the faults of other men, unless he feels truly that he is led
in this work, interiorly, by the Holy Spirit. Otherwise he may very
easily err in his judgments. And therefore, beware. Judge yourself
as you like—it is a matter between you and your God or between
you and your spiritual father—but leave other men alone.

Chapter 31

How to conduct oneself, when first
undertaking this exercise, against all sinful thoughts and impulses.

When once you feel that you have done all that is in your
power to make amends according to law by the judgment of
the holy church, then you must begin to dispose yourself
earnestly for the labor of this exercise. If it happens that particular sins which you have committed are always inserting themselves in your awareness between you and your God, or any
new thought or impulse concerning any other sin is, you are
bravely to step above it with a fervent impulse of love and tread
it down under your feet. And try to cover them with a thick
cloud of forgetting, as though they had never been committed
by you or by any other man. And if such thoughts often arise,
put them down often; in short, as often as they arise, as often put
them down. And if it seems to you that this is very laborious, you
can look for tricks and devices, secret subtleties and spiritual tactics, by which you can put them away. These tactics are better
learned from God than from the experience of any man in this
life.

Chapter 32

Two spiritual devices helpful to the
beginner in this exercise.

However, I would like to tell you something about these devices,
according to my experience. Put them to the test, and if you can
do any better, well and good.

You are to do all that in you lies to act as though you did not
know that they are pressing very hard upon you and coming
between you and your God. Try to look over their shoulders, as it
were, as though you were looking for something else: that
something else is God, surrounded on all sides by the cloud of
unknowing [cf. Exod. 20:21]. If you do this, I am sure that
within a short time you will find your burden easier. I believe
that when this device is well and truly understood, it is nothing
else but a longing desire for God, to experience him and see him
as far as may be possible here below. This desire is charity, and it
always wins easement.

There is another device which you can put to the test if you
so wish. When you feel that you can in no way put down these
thoughts, cower down under them like a poor wretch and a
coward overcome in battle and reckon it to be a waste of time
for you to strive any longer against them. In this way, though
you are in the hands of your enemies [cf. Jer. 12:7], you give
yourself up to God; feel as though you were hopelessly defeated.
Pay particular attention to this device, I pray you, for it seems to

me that when you put it to the test, you will find yourself melting as though to water [cf. Song of Sol. 5:4]. And truly it seems to me that if this device is properly understood in its subtlety, it is nothing else but a true knowledge and experience of yourself as you are, a wretch, filth, far worse than nothing [cf. 1 Cor. 1:28]. This knowing and experience is humility. This humility merits to have God himself coming down in his power to avenge you against your enemies, to take you up, to cherish you, and to dry your spiritual eyes [cf. Rev. 21:4; Isa. 61:3], as the father does for the child that was in danger of death under the mouths of wild boars or mad, biting bears.

Chapter 33

In this exercise a soul is absolved of his
particular sins and the punishment due
to them; and yet there is no perfect rest
in this life.

I am not going to speak to you of more devices at this time, for
if you have the grace to put these to the test by experience, I
believe that you will be able to teach me better than I can teach
you. And even though it might happen thus, truly it seems to me
that I am very far from arriving there. So I pray you to help me,
and work both on your own behalf and mine as well.

Press on, then, and labor earnestly for the time, I pray you.
Endure the pain humbly, if you cannot quickly acquire these
tricks. For truly this is your purgatory. But when your pain is all
over, and God has given you these devices, and you have acquired
the habit of them through grace, then I am sure that you will be
purified, not only from sin but also from the pain attaching to it.
I am speaking of the pain of your own special past sins, not of the
pain of original sin. For that will always be with you till your
dying day, no matter how earnestly you labor. Nevertheless it shall
trouble you little in comparison with the pain of your own particular sins. And even so, hard labor will always be yours. For new
and fresh impulses toward sinning are always springing up out of
this original sin, which you must always smite down and
earnestly cut away with the sharp, two-edged, awesome sword of

discretion [Heb. 4:12]. From this you can understand and learn that there is no absolute security or any true rest in this life. But you must not turn back because of this or be too fearsome of falling. For if it happens that you receive grace for the destruction of the pain of your own particular sins of the past, in the way I have described or better if you can, you may be sure that the pain of original sin, or else the new impulses to sin that are to come, will be able to trouble you hardly at all.

Chapter 34

God gives this grace freely and without
any preceding cause; it cannot be
achieved by any particular means.

If you ask me by what means you are to come to the practice of
this exercise, I beseech almighty God out of his great grace and
great courtesy to teach you himself [cf. John 6:45; Isa. 54:13].
For it is right for me to let you know that I cannot tell you. And
no wonder. Because this is work of God alone, brought about in
a special way in whatever soul that pleases him, without any
merit on its part. For without this divine work neither saint nor
angel can ever hope even to desire it. And I believe that our Lord
will deign to effect this work in those that have been habitual
sinners, particularly and as often, yes, and perhaps even more
particularly and more often, in those who have been habitual
sinners, than in others who, comparatively speaking, have never
caused him great grief. It is his will to do this because he wishes
to be seen as all-merciful and almighty; he wishes us to see that
he works as it pleases him and when it pleases him [cf. John 3:8].

At the same time, he does not give this grace or accomplish
this work in any soul who has not the capacity for it. And yet
there is no one lacking this grace who has not the capacity to
receive it, whether he be sinful or innocent. For the grace is not
given because of innocence, nor is it withheld because of sin. Take
careful notice that I say "withheld," not "withdrawn." You must

beware of error here; for the nearer we come to the truth, the more we must be on our guard against error, and this is my intention.

If you cannot understand what I say, lay it aside until God comes and teaches you. Do this, and keep out of harm's way. Be on your guard against pride, because it blasphemes God in his gifts and makes sinners arrogant. If you were truly humble, you would have the right feeling for this divine work, even as I say that God gives it freely without any meriting. The nature of the work is such that its presence gives the soul the capacity to possess it and to experience it; and no soul can have this capacity without that presence. The capacity for this exercise is inseparably united to the exercise itself. The two cannot be divided. So whoever experiences this divine work is able for it, otherwise not; insomuch that without this divine work a soul is, as it were, dead and cannot covet it or desire it. For as long as you have a will for it and a desire for it, insomuch you possess it, neither more nor less. Yet it is not a will or a desire, but something which you are at a loss to describe, which moves you to desire you know not what. You must not care if you understand no more of it; just press on with the exercise more and more, so that you are always engaged in it.

To put it more clearly, let it do with you and lead you as it will. Let it be the one that works; you simply must consent to it. Simply look at it, and just let it be. Do not interfere with it, as though you wished to help it on, lest you spill it all. Try to be the wood and let it be the carpenter; the house, and let it be the husbandman dwelling in the house. During this time be blind and cut away all desire of knowing, for this will hinder you more than it will help you. It is enough to know that you feel moved in love by something, though you do not know what it is, so that in the affection you have no thought of anything in particular under God, and that your reaching out is simply directed to God.

If this is the way of it, then trust steadfastly that it is God alone who moves your will and your desire: he alone, entirely of himself, without any intermediary either on his part or yours. And do not be afraid of the devil, for he cannot come so close. He can never come to move a man's will except very rarely and very indirectly, no matter how clever he is. Nor can a good angel move your will without an intermediary. In short, nothing can move it except God.

By what I have said here you may understand a little, but much more clearly by experience, that in this exercise men must use no intermediaries, nor can they come to it through intermediaries. All good intermediaries depend on it, but it depends on none of them; nor can any intermediary lead you to it.

Chapter 35

The threefold occupation of the contemplative apprentice: reading, reflecting, and praying.

Nevertheless, there are certain preparatory exercises which
should occupy the attention of the contemplative apprentice: the
lesson, the meditation, and the petition. They may be called, for a
better understanding, reading, reflecting, and praying. You will
find a much better treatment of these three than I can manage in
the book of another author. So I need not rehearse their qualities
here. I will, however, make the point—for those who are beginners and proficients, but not for the perfect, insofar as there are
such here below—that these three are so linked together that
there can be no profitable reflection without previous reading, or
hearing. (Reading and hearing come to the same thing: the clerics read the books, and the layfolk read the clerics when they listen to them preaching the word of God.) Nor will beginners or
proficients come to true prayer without previous reflection. See
how this is demonstrated in this same book.

God's word, whether written or spoken, is like a mirror. The
spiritual eye of your soul is your reason. Your spiritual face is
your consciousness. And just as your bodily eyes cannot see
where the dirty mark is on your bodily face without a mirror, or
without someone else telling you where it is, so with your spiritual faculties. Without reading or listening to God's word, it is

not possible for the understanding, when the soul is blinded by habitual sin, to see the dirty mark on his consciousness. It follows, then, that when a person sees in the bodily or the spiritual mirror, or knows by the information he gets from someone else, just where the dirty mark is on his bodily or spiritual face, he goes to the well to wash it off—and not before. Now if this mark is a particular sin, the well is the holy church and the water is confession, with all its elements. And if the mark is simply the blind root with the impulse to sin, then the well is the merciful God and the water is prayer, with all its elements.

And so you can see that beginners and proficients cannot come to proper reflection without previous reading or listening, or to prayer without previous reflection.

Chapter 36

The meditations of those habitually
occupied in the exercise described in
this book.

However, things are different for those habitually occupied in the
exercise described in this book. Their meditations are, so to
speak, sudden awarenesses and obscure feelings of their own
wretchedness or of God's goodness, without any previous reading or listening or of a special sight of anything under God.
These sudden intuitions and obscure feelings are more quickly
learned from God than from man.

It would not bother me at all if at this time your meditations on
your own sinfulness or God's goodness—given, of course, that
you feel yourself moved to it by grace in accord with your spiritual
counseling—amounted to nothing other than what you find in
the word "sin" or "God" or some similar word which took your
fancy. For here it is not a question of analyzing or elucidating these
words rationally or listing their various meanings in the hope that
such consideration would increase your devotion. I do not believe
this to be so, or that it could ever happen in this exercise. These
words must be held in their wholeness. By "sin" you must mean
some sort of undefined lump—nothing else, in fact, than yourself.
It is my belief that in this obscure looking at sin, as a congealed
mass which is none other than yourself, there should be no need
to look for anything to hold down during this time more irrational

than yourself. And yet anybody looking at you would see you quite coordinated in your bodily movements and nothing remarkable in the way you kept your countenance, whether you were sitting, walking, lying down or leaning on something, or standing or kneeling—sober and restful.

Chapter 37

The special prayers of the habitual workers in the exercise of this book.

Just as the meditations of those habitually exercised in this grace
and in this book are sudden intuitions without previous causes, it
is the same with their prayers. I am speaking of their personal
prayer and not of those ordained by the holy church. For those
who are truly exercised in this work have more regard for the
church's prayers than for any other, and they perform them in
the manner and according to the rubrics ordained by the holy
fathers who have gone before us. Their personal prayers, however, always rise directly to God without any intermediaries or
previous or concomitant meditation. And if words are used—and
this happens rarely—they are very few indeed; in fact, the fewer
the better. And it is my belief that a little word of one syllable is
better than of two and is more in accordance with the work of
the spirit. This is because a spiritual worker in this exercise
should always find himself at the supreme and sovereign point of
the spirit.

Let me explain the truth of this by taking as an example a natural event. When a man or a woman is suddenly seized with fear of
fire or of death or some similar happening, that person is suddenly smitten in the depths of his spirit to cry out and beg for
help. And he does this not in many words or even in one word of
two syllables. And this is because he feels that this would take too

long to give vent to his need and the laboring of his spirit. So he breaks out in a loud and hideous scream, using a little word of one syllable such as "Fire!" or "Out!"

Just as this little word "fire" suddenly beats upon and jars most effectively the ears of the bystanders, it is the same with the little word, whether spoken or thought or even obscurely conceived in the depth, or we may call it the height, of the spirit. (In the spiritual realm, height and depth, length and breadth are all the same.) And thus it bursts upon the ears of almighty God much more than any long psalm mumbled away in an inarticulate fashion. And this is why it is written that a short prayer pierces heaven [cf. Matt. 6:7].

Chapter 38

How and why their short prayer pierces
heaven.

Why does this little prayer of one syllable pierce the heavens?
Surely because it is offered with a full spirit, in the height and
the depth, in the length and the breadth of the spirit of him who
prays. In the height: that is with the full might of the spirit; in
the depth: for in this little syllable all the faculties of the spirit are
contained; in the length: because if it could always be experienced as it is in that moment, it would cry as it does then; in the
breadth: because it desires for all others all that it desires for
itself. It is in this moment that the soul comprehends with all the
saints what is the length and the breadth, the height and the
depth of the everlasting, all-loving, almighty, and all-wise God, as
St. Paul teaches, not fully, but in some way and to some degree,
as is proper to this work.

The eternity of God is his length, his love is his breadth, his power
is his height, and his wisdom is his depth [Eph. 3:18–19]. No wonder, then, that the soul which is so nearly conformed by grace to the
image and likeness of God his maker is immediately heard by God
[cf. 2 Cor. 3:18]. Yes, and even if it were a very sinful soul, one which
is, as it were, God's enemy, as long as it should come, through grace,
to cry out with such a little syllable from the height and the depth,
the length and the breadth of its spirit, it would always be heard and
helped by God in the very vehemence of its shriek.

Let us take an example. If a man happened to be your deadly enemy and you heard him cry out with such terror, in the fullness of his spirit, this little word "Fire!" or this word "Out!" you would have no thought for his enmity, but out of the heartfelt compassion, stirred up and excited by the pain expressed in that cry, you would get out of bed even on a night in midwinter to help him put out the fire or to bring him comfort in his distress. O Lord, if a man can be moved by grace to such mercy and compassion for his enemy, his enmity notwithstanding, what compassion and what mercy will God have, for the spiritual cry of the soul, welling up and issuing forth from the height and the depth, the length and the breadth of his spirit, which contains by nature all that a man has by grace, and much more! Surely he shall receive much more mercy, without comparison, since it follows that whatever belongs to a thing by nature is much closer to it than anything belonging to it by grace.

Chapter 39

How the perfect contemplative must pray; the nature of prayer in itself; if it is vocal, it must be appropriate to the nature of prayer.

We must therefore pray in the height and the depth, the length and the breadth of our spirit; and not in many words, but in a little word of one syllable. What shall this word be? Surely one which is most in accordance with the nature of prayer. What word is that? First, let us see what is the nature of prayer in itself, and then we can more clearly understand what word will be best in accordance with the nature of prayer.

Prayer in itself is nothing but a devout reaching out directly to God in order to attain the good and to do away with evil. And since every evil is comprehended in sin, either as its effect or as sin itself, when we wish to pray with concentration for the removal of evil, we must neither say nor think nor mean anything else, using no other words but this little word "sin." And if we desire with all our intent to pray for the attainment of any good, let us cry either verbally or in thought or desire, using nothing else, no other word, but this word "God." Because in God is contained all good, both as effect and as Being.

Do not wonder why I set these words above all others. If I could think of any shorter words which so completely contained in themselves all good and all evil as do these two words, or if

God taught me to use any other words, I would take them and leave these two; so I give you the same advice. But do not begin to reflect upon words, for if you do, you will never achieve your purpose or accomplish this work; for it is achieved not by reflection, but only by grace. So take no other words for your prayer, although I give these two examples, except those to which God moves you. At the same time, if God does move you to take these, I advise you not to leave them: I mean, if you must pray in words and not otherwise. Because these are very short words.

At the same time, although short prayers are highly recommended here, no bounds are being set on the frequency of prayer. For, as we have said, prayer is made in the length of the spirit. It must never end until what we long for is fully achieved. We have an example of this in the terror of the man or the woman of whom we have spoken before. We see that they never cease to cry out with this little word "out" or this little word "fire" until they have, by and large, been rescued from their affliction.

Chapter 40

During the time of this exercise, the
soul must pay no heed to any particular
vice or virtue or to the nature of either.

So, in the same way, you are to fill your spirit with the spiritual meaning of this word "sin," but without concentrating on any particular kind of sin, whether venial or grievous: pride, anger, envy, covetousness, sloth, gluttony, or lust. What does it matter to a contemplative what sin it is, or how great a sin it is? For it seems to him, during the time of this exercise, that every sin is as great as another, since the smallest sin separates him from God and is an obstacle to his inward peace.

So feel sin as a lump; never mind what it is, it is nothing else but yourself. Cry out spiritually always with the same cry, "Sin, sin, sin," "Out, out, out." This spiritual cry is better taught by God by experience than by the words of man. Its perfection consists in pure spirit, when there is no particular thought or any word pronounced, though it can happen occasionally that, because of the fullness of spirit, it bursts forth into words, for both body and soul are filled with sorrow and the heaviness of sin.

Do exactly the same with this little word "God." Fill your spirit with its spiritual meaning without concentrating particularly on any of his works, whether they be good, better, or best, physically or spiritually. Pay no regard either to any virtue that can be effected in man's soul by grace, whether this be humility or charity, patience or abstinence, hope, faith or temperance, chastity or voluntary poverty. What do all these matter to contemplatives? All virtues they find and experience in God, for in him is everything, both by cause and by being. And it seems to them that if they had God, then they would have all good. So they fix their desire on nothing in particular, but only on the good God. You are to do likewise insofar as you can by grace. Have God alone for your intention and only God; let neither your understanding nor your will have any object except God alone.

But since you must always experience in some measure, as long as you are living in this wretched life, this foul, stinking lump of sin, as it were, joined to and congealed with the substance of your being, you must fix your intention on one of these two words alternatively, "sin" and "God," with this vague knowledge: that if you had God, then you would be without sin, and if you were without sin, then you could have God.

Chapter 41

Discretion applies to all other exercises
except this.

If you ask me the further question how you are to apply discretion to this exercise, I answer and say, "None at all!" In all your other activities you are to have discretion, in eating and drinking, in sleeping, and in protecting your body from the extremes of heat and cold, in the length of time you give to prayer or reading or to conversation with your fellow Christians. In all these things you are to observe moderation, avoiding excess and defect. But in this exercise there is no question of moderation; I would prefer that you should never leave off as long as you live.

I do not say that you should persevere in it with the same vigor, for that is not possible. Sometimes sickness or other disorders of body or of soul and many other necessities of nature will greatly hinder you and often pull you down from the height of this exercise. But I do say that you should always be either doing it or preparing for it, that is to say, either actually or in intention. So, for the love of God, beware of sickness as much as it is possible for you. Insofar as you can, never be the cause of your physical weakness. For it is true what I say: this work demands a great tranquillity and a clean bill of health as well in body as in soul. So for the love of God, govern yourself wisely in body and in soul, and keep in good health as much as possible. But if sickness comes to attack your bodily strength, have patience and wait in humility for God's mercy [cf. Jude 21]. Everything shall then be well enough. What I say is true, that often patience in sickness and in various other tribulations [cf. 2 Cor. 6:4–5] pleases God much more than any satisfying devotion that you might have while you are in good health.

Chapter 42

Through lack of discretion in this exercise, we achieve discretion in all things,
and certainly in no other way.

Now perhaps you will ask how you shall observe prudence in eating and sleeping and everything else. My answer to this is brief enough: "Understand it as best you can." Work at this exercise without ceasing and without moderation, and you will know where to begin and to end all your other activities with great discretion. I cannot believe that a soul who perseveres in this exercise night and day without moderation should ever make a mistake in any of his external activities; but otherwise it seems to me that he can never be free of error. If I could only concentrate with earnestness and a vigilance on this spiritual exercise within my soul, I would be completely heedless about eating, drinking, speaking, and all other outward activities. For I am sure that I would rather arrive at discretion in them by this heedlessness than by any earnest consideration of them with the purpose of achieving a target or a degree of moderation in this respect. Indeed, I would never achieve it, no matter what I did or said. Other men may express different opinions, but experience is a true witness. So lift up your heart with this dark impulse of love; mean now "sin" and now "God." God you wish to have, and sin you would avoid. You lack God, but you are sure you have sin. Now may the good God help you, for here you have need!

Chapter 43

All awareness and experience of one's
own being must be done away with
before the perfection of this exercise be
truly experienced in this life.

Permit nothing to work in your understanding or in your will
except God alone. Try to destroy all understanding and awareness of anything under God, and tread everything down deep
under the cloud of forgetting. Understand that in this exercise
you are to forget all other creatures besides yourself, or their
deeds or yours; and in this exercise, you must also forget yourself and your own activities as well as all other creatures and
their activities, because of God. For the perfect lover's way is not
only to love the thing that he loves more than himself; he must
also, in a sense, hate himself for the sake of the thing that he
loves.

This, then, must be your attitude: every object that exercises
your understanding and your will you must account as loathsome
and wearisome, except God alone. For no matter what it is, it is certainly between you and your God. So it is no wonder that you
should loathe and hate to reflect on yourself, since you must always
experience sin as some sort of foul, fetid lump between yourself
and your God. This lump is nothing else than yourself; it shall seem
to you that it is one with, congealed with, the substance of your
being, as though there were no division between them.

So you must destroy all knowing and feeling of every kind of creature, but most especially of yourself. For on the knowledge and experience of yourself depends the knowledge and experience of all other creatures; compared with the self, all other creatures can easily be forgotten. If you are willing to make serious trial of this, you will find, after you have forgotten all other creatures and all their works, yes indeed and your own works as well, what remains between you and your God is a simple knowing and feeling of your own being. This knowing and feeling must always be destroyed, before it is possible for you to experience in truth the perfection of this exercise.

Chapter 44

How the soul must dispose itself to sup-
press all awareness and experience of its
own being.

Next you will ask me how you can destroy this simple awareness
and experience of your own being. For doubtless it seems to you
that, once it is destroyed, all other hindrances will be destroyed as
well. If this is what you think, you are certainly right. My answer
to you is this: without a very special grace which God gives out
of his absolute bounty, and along with it a corresponding capacity
on your part for receiving this grace, this simple awareness and
experience of your being can in no way be destroyed.

This capacity is nothing else but a strong and profound spiritual
sorrow. With regard to this sorrow you need to have this particular
discretion: you must take care, while you have this sorrow, not to
put too great a strain on your body or your spirit, but to keep very
still, as though you were asleep, all worn out and sunk deep in this
sorrow [cf. Luke 22:45]. Here is true sorrow; here is perfect sorrow.
He is fortunate, indeed, who can come to this sorrow. All men have
reason for sorrow, but he who knows and feels that he exists has a
very special experience of sorrow.

In comparison to this, all other sorrows seem to be a sort of pretense. Certainly, he who is aware and experiences not only what he
is but that he is can sorrow in earnest. But he who has no experience
of this sorrow, let him begin to make sorrow, because he is not yet

experienced in perfect sorrow. This sorrow and the possession of it purifies a man's soul not only of sin, but also of the punishment that he has deserved because of his sin. It thus makes it possible for the soul to receive that joy which takes away all a man's awareness and experience of his own being.

This sorrow, if we understand it aright, is full of holy desires. Otherwise, in this life a man could never abide it or bear it. For unless a man were to be sustained in some way with some consolation in the true performance of this exercise, he would not be able to bear the pain which he has from the awareness and experience of his own being. For often he desires to have a true awareness and experience of God in purity of spirit, as far as this is possible in this life; and as often he feels that he cannot, because he always finds that his awareness and experience are in a sense occupied and filled with this foul and fetid lump of himself. And because this lump must always be hated and despised and forsaken, if a man would be God's perfect disciple and taught by him on the mountain of perfection, he is nearly out of his mind with sorrow [cf. Matt. 26:37–38]; so much so that he weeps and wails, strives with himself, denounces and heaps curses upon himself. In a word, it seems to him that this burden of himself which he carries is so heavy that he does not care what happens to him, as long as God is pleased.

At the same time, in all this sorrow he has no desire not to be, because that would be the devil's madness and contempt for God. Rather, he is very glad to be, and he is sincere in his heartfelt thanks to God for the noble gift of his being, although he desires, without seeking, to lose the awareness and experience of his being.

Every soul must possess and experience in itself this sorrow and this desire, either in this way or in another way as God will grant in the teaching of his spiritual disciples, according to his good pleasure and their corresponding capacity, in body and in soul, in degree and disposition, before they can be perfectly united to God in perfect charity, insofar as this union can be possessed in this life, if God will grant it.

Chapter 45

A detailed explanation of certain illusions that can occur during this exercise.

Let me tell you something else. During this exercise, it is very easy
for a young disciple who is not yet accustomed to spiritual exercises and is little experienced in them to be deceived. Unless he is
aware of this from the start and has the grace to stop and submit
himself to spiritual direction, it is likely that his bodily strength will
be seriously damaged, and he will become the victim of spiritual
illusion. All this is due to pride and sensuality and false reasoning.

This illusion can happen in the following way. When young men
or women who are beginners in the school of devotion hear this
sorrow and this desire read or spoken about, how a man must lift up
his heart to God and desire without ceasing to experience the love
of his God, then, straightaway, in their false reasoning they understand these words not as they are meant, spiritually, but carnally and
physically, and they strive in their foolishness to raise up the heart in
their breasts. And because grace is lacking to them, as they deserve
for their pride and false reasoning, they strain themselves and their
physical strength so roughly and so stupidly that within a short time
they fall victim to weariness or to a languid weakness in body and
in soul, which tempts them to go out of themselves and to seek
some false and empty sensible and physical comfort outside for the
relaxation of body and spirit. Or, if they do not fall victim to this,
through their spiritual blindness and the way in which they play on

their sensations during the time of this false, animal, and far from spiritual exercise, it is likely that their hearts will be inflamed with an unnatural fervor due to the way in which they treat their bodies or to this false exercise, or else there is created in their imagination a false heat, the work of the devil, their ghostly enemy. And all this comes from their pride, their earthliness, and their false reasoning.

Yet, like as not, they think that this is a fire of love produced and kindled by the grace and the goodness of the Holy Spirit. From such illusions as these and their ramifications come great mischief, great hypocrisy, great heresy, and great error. For after the illusions in their feelings, there immediately follows a deception in knowing which belongs to the devil's school, in the same way as a true knowledge in God's school follows immediately on a true experience. For it is true that the devil has his contemplatives even as God has his. This deceit and illusion in feeling, and in the awareness which follows upon it, has many different and remarkable variations according to the different states and conditions of those that are deceived; as many as there are among those who, having true experience and awareness, are in a healthy state.

But I will not set down here any further examples of illusions, only those with which I believe you will be assailed whenever you set yourself to do this exercise. For what profit would it be to you to know how learned theologians and men and women in states of life other than your own suffer illusion? Truly, none. That is why I speak of no others than those which might happen to you when you set yourself to this exercise. And I am telling you about them so that you can be on your guard against them in your own exercise, if you are affected in this way.

Chapter 46

A careful instruction on how to avoid these illusions; the exercise demands spiritual zest rather than bodily exertion.

So, for the love of God, take very great care in this exercise not to strain yourself immoderately or overtax the heart in your breast. The exercise calls for spiritual skill rather than brute strength. To work more skillfully means to work with humility and in the spirit; if you force it, the work is merely in the body and the senses. So take care. For, indeed, if one should presume to draw near to the high mountain of this exercise in a beastlike way, one shall be driven away with stones [cf. Heb. 12:20]. It is the nature of stones to be dry and hard, and where they strike, there one feels it sorely. These physical exertions are very firmly fixed to the sensible feelings, and they are very dry in that they lack the dew of grace. So they hurt the foolish soul very sorely, and the illusion caused by fiends makes the wound fester.

So beware of these beastlike efforts and learn to love with true fervor, with a gentle and peaceful disposition, both in body and soul [cf. Matt. 11:28–30]. And wait patiently on the will of our Lord with courtesy and humility [cf. Hab. 2:3; Ps. 27:14], and do not snatch at it hurriedly, like a greedy greyhound, no matter how hungry you may be. And I advise you to play some sort of game, so that you can do all that is possible to contain these great and boisterous movements of your spirit, as though you did not wish him to know in any way how you desire to see him and have him or experience him. Perhaps you think this is somewhat foolishly and childishly spoken. But I am certain that whoever had the grace to do and feel as I say would find that this game was well worth playing, as the father plays with the child, kissing and embracing it.

Chapter 47

A careful instruction on the purity of
spirit demanded in this exercise: how
the soul must make its desire known to
God in one way and to man in quite a
different way.

Do not be surprised at my speaking in this apparently childish
and foolish way, as though I were lacking normal discretion. I do
it for several reasons, for I believe that I have been led for a long
time now to feel and to think and also to speak in this way to
others of my special friends in God as I am now speaking to you.

One reason why I bid you hide the desire of your heart from
God is this. I hope that by such concealment it may become more
clearly known to him, to your advantage and for the fulfillment of
this very desire, than it would be by any other way that I believe
to be within your power of making it known to him. A further
reason is that I wish, through this concealed showing, to bring
you out of the ignorant state of sensible feeling into the purity
and depth of spiritual feeling, and so finally to help you to fasten
the spiritual knot of burning love between you and your God in
spiritual oneness and union of wills.

Of this you are well aware, that God is a spirit. And whoever
wishes to be made one with him must live in the truth and depth
of spirit, far removed from any bodily travesty of it. It is true also
that everything is known to God and nothing can be hid from his

knowing [cf. Luke 12:2; John 21:17; Ps. 44:21], whether it be sensible or spiritual. But since it is also true that he is a spirit, then that which is hid in the depths of the spirit is known and shown to him more openly than anything which is in any way contaminated by the senses. For in the natural order of things, that which is sensible is farther from God than that which is spiritual. For this reason it appears that as long as our desire is contaminated with any kind of sensible thing, as it is when we strive and strain in spirit and body together, then for that time it is farther off from God than it should be if it were done with more devotion and more zeal, in tranquillity, and in the purity and depth of the spirit.

This will help you to understand to some extent the reason why I ask you to conceal and to hide from God in this childish way the movement of your desire. But I do not bid you simply to hide it, for it would be the command of a fool to bid you do something that simply cannot be done in any way. I ask you to take every step that you can to hide it. And why do I command you thus? Simply because I want you to put it down into the depths of your spirit, far from any ignorant contamination with any sensible thing which would make it less spiritual, and in that far, so much farther away from God. I am sure as well that the more truly refined your spirit is, the less it is contaminated by the sensible and the nearer it is to God, the better it pleases him, and the more clearly it may be seen by him. This is not to say that his sight may be at one time or in respect of one object more clear than at another, for it is always unchangeable; but because, when the object is in purity of spirit, it is more like to him, who is a spirit.

There is another reason why I bid you to do all that in you lies to keep this desire hidden from him. You and I, and many others like us, are so inclined to conceive of the spiritual in a sensible way that perhaps, had I directed you to show to God the movement of your heart, you would have showed it to him in a sensible way, either by a look or an exclamation or a word or some other ignorant sensible effort, as happens when you wish to reveal what is hidden in your heart to another man. And had this happened, your exercise would have been impure. For in one way must things be shown to man, and in another to God.

Chapter 48

God wishes to be served with both
body and soul, and to reward man
in both; and how we may know when
the sounds and sweetnesses affecting
the bodily senses in time of prayer are
good, and when evil.

When I say this, it is not my meaning that you should leave off at
any time, if you are moved to pray in words or suddenly to break
out because of the devotion in your spirit, to speak to God as to
man and to speak, as you feel yourself moved to do, such good
words as these: "Good Jesus, lovely Jesus, sweet Jesus," and so
on. No, God forbid that you should take it so, for I do not mean
it in this way at all. God also forbid that I should separate what
he has joined together, the body and the spirit; for it is God's
will to be served both in body and soul together as is seemly,
and to give man his reward, in bliss, both in body and in soul.

As a pledge of that reward, it is sometimes his will to set on fire
the bodily senses of his devout servants here in this life, and not
once or twice but perhaps very often and according to his pleasure, with marvelous sweetness and consolation. Such consolations
as these do not come into our bodies from without through the
windows of our senses, but they come from within, rising and
springing up out of the abundance of spiritual gladness and of
true devotion in the spirit. Such comfort and sweetness should not

be held suspect; and to be brief, I believe that he who has this experience cannot hold it suspect.

But the consolations, sounds, gladness, and sweetness which come suddenly from outside, even though you do not know whence, I beseech you to hold all these suspect, for they can be either good or evil. If they are good, they are produced by a good angel, and if bad, then by an evil angel. They cannot be evil as long as those illusions arising from false reasoning and immoderate effort of the heart and senses are removed, according to my instruction, or better instruction, if you can get it. And why is that? Because of the cause of this comfort, which is the devout stirring of love which dwells in pure spirit. It comes from the hand of almighty God without any intermediary; and therefore it must always be far removed from any illusion or false opinion that can come upon a man in this life.

It is not my intention at this time to tell you how to distinguish whether those other comforts and sounds and sweetness are good or evil. And the reason is that I do not think that it is necessary, because you can find it written down in another place in another man's book a thousand times better than I can say or write it. And there you can also find what I am setting down here, said in a far better way than I do here. But I will not on that account forbear, nor shall it weary me, to fulfill the desire and the movement of your heart which you have previously shown me in your words, and now in your deeds.

This is what I say, then, about those sounds and that sweetness which come in by the window of your senses, which can be either good or evil. Exercise yourself constantly in this simple, devout, zealous stirring of love of which I have been speaking. Then I have no doubt that this will be well able to tell you about them. Even if at first it is in some way or other dumbfounded by them, because it is not used to them, yet it will do this for you: it will bind your heart so strongly that you will not be able in any way to give any real credence to them until you are assured of their authenticity by the Spirit of God, inwardly in wondrous manner, or else outwardly, by the counsel of a spiritual father who has discretion.

Chapter 49

> The substance of all perfection is nothing
> else but a good will; and how all the sen-
> sible sounds, consolations, and sweetness
> that affect us in this life are accidental to
> this perfection.

I pray you, then, to follow eagerly after this humble stirring of love in your heart. It will be your guide in this life and bring you to grace in the next. It is the substance of all good living, and without it no good work can be begun or ended. It is nothing else but a good will that is directed to God, and a kind of satisfaction and gladness that you experience in your will concerning all that he does.

This good will is the substance of all perfection. All sweetnesses and consolations, sensible or spiritual, no matter how holy, are accidentals of this good will; they depend on it.

I call them its accidentals, for they can be present or absent without doing it much damage. I am speaking, of course, of this life. It is otherwise in the happiness of heaven, for there they will be united with the substance without any separation, even as the body in which they are experienced will be united with the soul. Their substance here is this good spiritual will. And I am sure that for him who experiences the perfection of this will, insofar as it may be possessed here, there is no sweetness or consolation which can come to any man in this life which he is not as equally pleased and glad to do without as he is to have, if it is in accordance with God's will.

Chapter 50

What chaste love is; and how sensible
consolations come very seldom to some
creatures, but very often to others.

You can see, then, that we must focus all our attention on this
meek stirring of love in our will. And with regard to all other
sweetnesses and consolations, sensible or spiritual, no matter
how pleasing they are, no matter how holy, we should have a
sort of heedlessness, if this can be said without failing in
courtesy and seemliness. If they come, welcome them, but do
not depend too much on them because of your weakness; for
to continue for long in those sweet experiences and tears is a
great drain on your strength. It may be that you will be moved
to love God simply for their sake. You will know that this is so if
you grumble overmuch when they are withdrawn. If this is your
experience, then your love is not yet either chaste or perfect. For
when love is chaste and perfect, though it is content that the
bodily senses be nourished and consoled through the presence
of these experiences and tears, yet it does not grumble. It is well
satisfied to do without them, if such be God's will.

Some people are normally never without such comforts,
but for others such sweetnesses and consolations occur very
seldom. It depends entirely on the disposition and the ordinance of God, who looks to the different advantages and needs
of his creatures. Some of them are so weak and so delicate in

spirit that unless they were comforted somewhat by experiencing such sweetness, they could not at all abide or put up with the various temptations and tribulations with which they are burdened in this life at the hands of their bodily and spiritual enemies. There are some whose bodily health is so poor that they are unable to do penance for their own purification. It is the Lord's will to purify such people with his great graces in spirit by these sweet consolations and tears. Again, on the other hand, there are some who are so strong in spirit that they have consolation enough interiorly, within their souls, in offering up this reverent and humble stirring of love and union of wills, so that they scarcely need to be sustained with these sweet consolations in their bodily senses. Now which of these two kinds is holier or pleasing to God, God alone knows, and not I.

Chapter 51

> We should be greatly on our guard not
> to interpret in a physical way what is to
> be understood in a spiritual way, and
> especially the words "in" and "up."

So follow humbly this simple stirring of love in your heart; I do not mean in your physical heart, but in your spiritual heart, which is your will. And take great care that you do not construe in a material way what is to be understood spiritually. For what I say is true: that the material and sensual interpretations of those who go in for elaborate whims and fancies are the cause of much error.

One example of this you can see in my asking you to conceal your desire from God insofar as you can. For perhaps had I asked you to show your desire to God, you would have interpreted this in a more material way than you do now, when I have bidden you hide it. You are well aware that whatever is deliberately concealed is sunk deep into your spirit.

So it seems to me that we need to be greatly on our guard in the interpretation of words which are spoken with spiritual intent, lest we interpret them in a material way and not spiritually, as they are meant. It is particularly important to be careful about this word "in" and this word "up," because the misinterpretation of these two words is the cause of much error and much illusion in those who set themselves to these spiritual exercises, or so it seems to me. I know this partly by experience and partly by hearsay. And I would like to give you a brief description of these illusions.

The young disciple in God's school, newly converted from the world, may think that because he has for a short while given himself to penance and to prayer according to the advice received in confession, he is therefore able to take upon himself these spiritual exercises which he hears spoken about, or hears read, or perhaps reads himself. Now when he reads or hears these spiritual exercises spoken of, and particularly how a man must draw all his understanding within himself, or how he should rise above himself, then straightaway, because of his soul's blindness and his sensuality and natural acumen, he misunderstands what is said. And because he has within him a natural desire to discover what is hidden, he concludes that he is called by grace to this exercise. The result is that, if his spiritual director is unwilling to agree that he should undertake this exercise, immediately the disciple feels badly disposed to his spiritual director and believes and perhaps even says to others who are in the same state as himself that he can find no one who can understand what he really means. And so, without any hesitation, because of the arrogance and presumption which comes from his intellectual pride, he abandons humble prayer and penance far too early and sets himself, or so he thinks, to true spiritual exercises within his soul. Such exercise, if it be rightly understood, is the work neither of the senses nor of the spirit. In a word, it is an unnatural activity, and the devil is its architect. Here is the quickest way to death both of body and of soul, for it is madness and not wisdom, and leads a man to madness. But the young disciple does not think in this way, for it is his intent in such an exercise to think of nothing except God.

Chapter 52

How young beginners in their presumption misinterpret this word "in,"
and the illusions which follow from
this.

The madness of which I spoke above comes about in this way.
They read and hear it said that they are to leave off the outward
exercise of their senses and work interiorly; and because they are
ignorant of what interior working means, they therefore work
wrongly. They turn their bodily senses inwards on themselves,
physically, which is unnatural. They strain themselves, as though
they could possibly see inwardly with their bodily eyes and hear
inwardly with their ears, and so with all their senses of smell, of
taste, and of touch. And so they reverse the order of nature; they
so overtax their imagination with this fantastic behavior and
without the least discretion, that finally they turn their brains in
their heads.

The result is that the devil has power to fabricate false lights or
sounds, sweet smells in their nostrils, wonderful tastes in their
mouths and many other strange ardors and burnings in their
bodily breasts or in their entrails, in their backs and their kid-
neys, and in their private parts. And yet in spite of this illusion,
they believe that they have a tranquil awareness of their God
without any hindrance of vain thoughts. And, indeed, they have
in a certain sense, because they are so filled with falsehood that

idle thoughts cannot afflict them. And why? Because the same devil who would afflict them with idle thoughts, were they in a good state, is the chief architect in this work; and you know well enough that he is in no hurry to hinder himself. He will not drive away the awareness of God from them, for fear that they should suspect that he is at work.

Chapter 53

The various kinds of unseemly outward
behavior of those who have no experience in this exercise.

Those who are so deceived as to take up this false exercise, or
any species of it, are addicted to much strange behavior in comparison with those who are God's true disciples. These latter are
always very decorous in their way of governing themselves,
either physically or spiritually. But it is not so of the others. Whoever might happen to catch sight of them and of their behavior
at the time when their eyes are wide open will see them staring
like madmen do, looking as though they were seeing the devil.
And, indeed, they had better beware, for the devil indeed is not
very far away. The eyes of some of them are so set in their heads
as though they were sheep suffering from the brain disease and
were near death's door. Some of them hold their heads on one
side as though a worm were in their ears. Some squeak instead
of speaking normally, as though there were no breath in their
bodies. Hypocrites tend to behave like this. Some, again, are so
eager and quick to say what they think that they gurgle and
splutter in their throats, which is what heretics are wont to do,
and those who with their presumption and cleverness stub-
bornly hold fast to their error [cf. Prov. 6:12–13].

Many disordered and unseemly gestures result from false opinion,
as anyone can see. At the same time, some of them are so clever that

they can for the most part control themselves when they are in anyone's company. But if you could see them in their own houses, then
I am sure that they could not hide their faults. Nevertheless, I think
that if anyone were to contradict their opinions, they would see
them react in some way or other. For in spite of everything they are
sure that all they do is for the love of God and to maintain the truth.
My expectation is that they are likely to go on loving God in this
peculiar fashion until they go stark staring mad to the devil; unless,
that is, he shows them his marvelous mercy and makes them put an
end to this behavior.

I am not saying that there is anyone so perfect a servant of the devil
in this life as to be diseased and infected with all the fantasies that I
write down here. Yet at the same time it could be that someone, and
perhaps many, are infected with them all. What I do say is that there is
no thoroughgoing hypocrite or heretic in this life who is innocent of
all the fantastic behavior I have mentioned, or will mention, if God
gives me leave.

For some people are so burdened with quaint and unseemly
posturing in their behavior, that when they have to listen to
anything, they waggle their heads from side to side and up
and down most oddly. They gape with open mouths, as
though they are listening with them and not with their ears.
Others, when they have to speak, use their fingers, either pok-
ing on their own fingers or their chests or the chests of those
to whom they are speaking. Others yet can neither sit, stand,
nor lie still; they have to be tapping with their feet or doing
something with their hands. Some make rowing motions with

their arms while they speak, as though they were in for a long swim. Some are always laughing and smiling with every other word, as though they were girlish gossips or amateur jugglers unsure of their balance.

I am not saying that all this indecorous behavior is in itself great sin, or even that the perpetrators of it are great sinners. What I do say is that these unseemly and inordinate gestures have such control over the man that makes them that he cannot stop them even when he wants to. So I maintain that they are signs of pride, of outlandishness, of exhibitionism and an inordinate desire for knowledge. In particular they are true tokens of moral instability and mental restlessness, and they indicate a lack of acquaintance with the exercises described in this book. The reason why I mention so many of these illusions here in these chapters is that he who undertakes this exercise can consider them, if he will, in order to put his own work to the test.

Chapter 54

By means of this work a man learns to
govern himself wisely and decorously in
body and soul alike.

If a man were practiced in this exercise, it would give him true
decorum both of body and soul, and would make him truly
attractive to all men or women who looked upon him. So
much so that the most ill-favored man or woman alive, if they
could come by grace to work in this exercise, would suddenly
be changed in appearance to such graciousness that all good
people who saw them would wish and rejoice to have them in
their company, and would be convinced that they had found
spiritual peace and were strengthened in God's grace through
their presence.

So reach out for this gift, you who can do so by grace. Whoever truly possesses it will know well how to govern himself and
all that belongs to him by its power. He would be able to discern
properly, at need, every kind of natural behavior and disposition.
He would know how to make himself all things to all men who
lived with him [cf. 1 Cor. 9:19–22], whether habitual sinners or
not, without any sin on his own part [cf. Luke 15:1–2]. He would
be the wonder of all who saw him, and would draw others by the
help of grace to the work of that same spirit in which he himself
is exercised. His looks and his words would be full of spiritual
wisdom, full of fire and of fruitfulness, spoken with truth and

soberness, without any falsehood, far removed from any hypo-critical showing off or pretense [cf. 1 Cor. 13:4–6].

There are, however, others who study with all their might, inward and outward, how they can inflate themselves in their speech and prop themselves up on every side with many humble-sounding words and gestures of devotion. Their aim is to seem holy in the sight of men, rather than to be holy in the sight of God and his angels [cf. Luke 11:42–43; 18:9–14]. Such people care more and sorrow more for a disordered gesture or an unseemly and unfitting word spoken before men, than they do for a thousand idle thoughts and foul stirrings of sin deliber-ately accepted or carelessly committed in the sight of God and of the saints and angels of heaven. Ah, Lord God! Whether or not there is any pride within when such meek-sounding words are so plentiful without, I truly believe that it is fitting and seemly for those who are really humble within to show humble and seemly words and outward gestures which correspond to the humility within the heart. What I say is that this should not be shown in broken or in plaintive tones, contrary to the nor-mal and natural voice of the speaker. Because if the words are true, then they will be spoken in a truthful way, in a round tone, coming from the hearts of those that speak them. Now, if he who has a naturally round and resonant tone speaks poorly and pipingly, unless of course he has a physical defect or his way of speaking has to do with his relationship with God or with his confessor, then it is a true token of hypocrisy, whether the person be young or old.

What more must I say of these poisonous illusions? I truly believe that unless these people have the grace to leave off such whining hypocrisy, which is the link between the secret pride in their hearts within and their humble words without, their miserable souls will soon sink down into sorrow.

Chapter 55

To condemn sin without discrimination
through excessive fervor is erroneous.

The devil deceives other men in the following way. In quite a
remarkable fashion he sets their brains on fire for the maintenance
of God's law and the destruction of sin in all other men. He never
tempts them with anything that is openly evil. He makes them
behave like busy prelates, who watch over various states of life of
Christian men, or like an abbot over his monks. They reprove all
men of their faults, just as though they had the pastoral care of
their souls. Indeed, they hold that they dare not act otherwise
before God. So whatever faults they see in men, they tell them
about them, saying that they are moved to do this by the fire of
charity and of God's love in their hearts; but they are liars, for it is
rather by the fire of hell welling up in their brains and in their
imaginations. That this is true may be gathered from what follows.

The devil is a spirit, and according to his nature he has no
body, any more than an angel has; but at the same time, whenever
he or any angel by God's permission takes bodily appearance in
order to minister to any man in this life, his body is in some way
fashioned according to the work he has to do. We have examples
of this in holy Scripture. Whenever an angel was sent in bodily
appearance, in the Old Testament and also in the New, it was
always made clear, either by his name or by some function or
quality of his body, what the spiritual matter of his message was. It
is exactly the same with the devil. When he comes in bodily

appearance, he shows in some bodily quality the spiritual nature of his servants.

One example of this will stand for all others. I have learned from students of necromancy who make it their study to win the help of wicked spirits, and from others to whom the devil has appeared in bodily likeness, that no matter what bodily appearance the devil takes on, he always has only one nostril, which is large and wide. And he will willingly turn it up, so that a man can see up it into his brain. His brain is nothing else than the fire of hell, for the devil can have no other brain. And he seeks for nothing better than to make a man look into it, for in that sight he would lose his mind forever. But the perfect apprentice of necromancy knows this well enough, and can take the proper steps beforehand to avoid being harmed in this way.

It is for this reason that I say, and have said, that whenever the devil takes on any bodily appearance, he shows in some bodily quality what his servants are in spirit. He inflames the imagination of his contemplatives with the fire of hell, so that suddenly, without discretion, they give vent to their clever visionings and, without any sort of deliberation, take it upon themselves immediately to blame other men's faults. This is because they have only one spiritual nostril. The division in the nose that separates one nostril from the other indicates that a man should have spiritual discretion and be able to separate good from evil, evil from worse, and good from better before he makes any considered judgment of anything he hears or sees done or spoken around him. By a man's brain is spiritually understood the imagination, for it has its natural position and function in the head.

Chapter 56

To pay more attention to intellectual
acumen or to speculative theologians
than to the ordinary teaching and counsel of the holy church is erroneous.

There are others who, though they are not deceived by the illusion I have been mentioning, yet because of their pride and the
cleverness of their natural understanding and academic learning, desert the common teaching and counsel of the holy
church. These and all their followers incline too much to their
own opinion. Because they have not received the proper
grounding in this humble, simple experience and virtuous living, it is their lot to have false experience fabricated and devised
by the spiritual enemy, so that finally they break out and blas-
pheme all the saints, sacraments, laws, and ordinances of the
holy church. Men of the world who live according to the flesh,
who think that the laws of the holy church are too hard to live
by, incline themselves to these heretics very quickly and easily
and uphold them staunchly, simply because they believe that
they will lead them by an easier way than that of the holy
church.

My firm belief is that he who does not wish to go by the nar-
row way to heaven [Matt. 7:13–14] shall go the soft way to hell.
Let every man make test of this in himself. And I believe that all
these heretics and all their followers, if they could be seen as
clearly as they will appear on the last day, would straightway

appear burdened down by the great and horrible sins of the world and their foul flesh, quite apart from their open presumption in maintaining error. Truly, then, are they called the disciples of Antichrist, for it is said of them that, in spite of their outward appearance, secretly they are foul lechers.

Chapter 57

Young disciples in their presumption
misunderstand this other word "up";
and the illusions that follow from this.

Let us say no more about these people now, but get on with our subject: how these young, presumptuous spiritual disciples misunderstand this other word "up." When they read or hear read or spoken how men should lift up their hearts to God, they look up to the stars as though they would reach above the moon, and cock their ears as though they could hear angels sing out of heaven. In their fantastic imagination they would pierce the planets or make a hole in the firmament to look through it. They would fashion a God according to their own fancy, dress him in rich clothes, and set him on a throne far more fantastically than he was ever painted on this earth. They would fashion angels in bodily appearance and accoutre each one with different musical instruments, in far more curious detail than was ever heard of or seen in this life.

Some of these the devil will delude in a remarkable manner. He will send down a sort of dew, which they think to be angels' food, that appears to come out of the air and falls softly and sweetly into their mouths. And so it is their habit to sit with their mouths open as though they were catching flies. Now all this is in truth delusion, however pious it might appear; for on these occasions their souls are void of any true devotion. Great vanity and falsehood are in their hearts; and the cause is their outlandish exercises. So much so that very often the devil fabricates peculiar sounds in their ears, strange lights and shining in their eyes, and remarkable scents in their nostrils; but all is false.

Yet they do not think so. They believe that they are following the example of St. Martin. He, in his exercises, looked upward and saw, by revelation, God clad in his mantle among the angels; and also of St. Stephen, who saw our Lord standing in the heavens [Acts 7:55]; and of many others also; and of Christ himself, who ascended bodily into heaven in the sight of his disciples [Acts 1:9–11]. And so they say that we should turn our eyes upward. I certainly agree that if we are so moved in spirit, then in our outward behavior we should lift up our eyes and our hands. But I say that in our spiritual exercises we should not direct ourselves either upward or downward, or to one side or the other, or forward or backward, as one does in bodily matters. Because our exercise is a spiritual exercise and not a physical one, it is not to be performed in a physical way.

Chapter 58

St. Martin and St. Stephen are not to be
taken as examples of straining upward
in our sensible imagination during the
time of prayer.

And though it is true what they say of St. Martin and St. Stephen,
that they saw such events with their bodily eyes, these things
were shown to them by a miracle, an authentication of things
spiritual. They are well aware that the cloak of St. Martin was
never placed on Christ's shoulders in reality, as though he had
any need of it to keep him from the cold, but miraculously and
in appearance, for all our sakes who can be brought to salvation;
for we are made one with the body of Christ in spirit [Eph. 4:4].
Those who clothe a poor man or who do any other good work,
corporal or spiritual, for the love of God to any who are in need
may be sure that they do it spiritually for Christ, and they shall
be rewarded as fully as if they had done it to Christ in the flesh.
He says this himself in the gospel [Matt. 25:40]. Yet this was not
enough for him; he felt that he must prove it by working miracles. It is for this reason that he revealed himself as he did to St.
Martin.

All the revelations that were ever manifested in bodily likeness
to anyone here in this life have spiritual meaning. And my belief
is that if they to whom they were shown, or we for whose sake
they were shown, were spiritual enough and were thus able to

understand the spiritual meanings of these revelations, they would never have been manifested in bodily likeness. So let us strip off the rough shell and feed on the sweet kernel.

How are we to do this? Not as the heretics do, whom we may well compare to those wild men who, after drinking from a beautiful cup, have the custom of throwing it against the wall and breaking it. We should not imitate them, if we want to behave in a civilized fashion. We should not feed on the fruit and then despise the tree; nor should we drink and then break the cup after we have drunk. By the tree and the cup are to be understood these miracles that are visible and all those seemly bodily gestures that correspond with and do not hinder the work of the spirit. By the fruit and the drink are to be understood the spiritual meaning of these visible miracles and those seemly bodily gestures, such as lifting up our hands and our eyes to heaven. If they are done because the spirit so moves us, then they are well done; but otherwise they are hypocrisy and falsehood. If they are true and contain spiritual fruit within them, there is no reason why they should be despised, for men will kiss the cup on account of the wine that is in it.

What, though, of our Lord, who, when he had ascended bodily into heaven, went his way upward into the clouds in the sight of his mother and his disciples? Should we therefore in our spiritual exercises continue to stare upward with our bodily eyes, to look and see if we can see him sitting in the flesh in heaven or else standing as St. Stephen saw him? No, indeed. He did not reveal himself bodily in heaven to St. Stephen in order to leave us an example that in our spiritual exercises we should look up into heaven with our bodily eyes, in order that we might see him as did St. Stephen, either standing or sitting or lying down.

No one knows how his body is disposed in heaven, whether standing or sitting or lying down. Nor is it necessary to know this, nor anything else, except that his body has been raised on high with his soul without any division. His body and soul, which is his manhood, is made one with the Godhead without any separation. We need know nothing of his sitting or standing or lying down, but only this, that he is there present as pleases him, and he is so disposed in body as is most seemly for him to be. And if he shows himself lying down or standing or sitting in bodily fashion by revelation to any creature in this life, he does this for some spiritual meaning, not because of any disposition of body that he adopts in heaven.

Let us take an example. By "standing" is to be understood a readiness to help. So one friend is accustomed to say to another in time of battle: "Carry yourself well, man; fight hard and do not withdraw from the battle too easily; I will stand by you." By this is meant not merely a bodily standing by; for perhaps this battle is being fought on horseback and not on foot, and perhaps it is a running and not a standing fight. What he means when he says he will stand by his friend is that he shall be at hand to help him.

This was the reason our Lord showed himself in bodily appearance in heaven to St. Stephen when he was enduring martyrdom, not to give us an example that we should look up into heaven. It was as though he said to St. Stephen, as the representative of all those who suffer persecution for God's love: "See, Stephen, I am opening this physical firmament, which is called heaven, to let you see me standing there. So you must trust steadfastly that as truly do I stand beside you spiritually, by the power of my Godhead, and am at hand to help you. Stand then bravely in the faith and endure steadfastly the severe buffetings of these hard stones. For your reward I shall crown you in bliss; and not you alone, but all those who suffer persecution in any way for my sake." So you can see that the purpose of these bodily showings was for their spiritual meaning.

Chapter 59

The bodily ascension of Christ is not to be taken as an example of straining upwards in our sensible imagination in time of prayer; time, place, and the body are all to be forgotten during this spiritual exercise.

If you say, concerning the ascension of our Lord, that it took place bodily and for a bodily purpose as well as for a spiritual one, because he ascended as true God and true man, my answer is that he had been dead and was clothed in immortality [cf. 1 Cor. 15:52–53], as we too shall be at the last day. Then we shall be so subtle in body and soul together that we shall be able to move bodily wheresoever we wish, as swiftly as we can now move spiritually in our thoughts, whether up or down, to one side or the other, behind or in front. And I expect that then every movement will be equally good, as the theologians say. But now you cannot come up to heaven bodily, but only spiritually; and this movement is to be so spiritual that it can have nothing to do with bodily movement, neither up nor down, to one side or the other, behind or in front.

You must realize that all those who devote themselves to spiritual exercises, and particularly the exercises described in this book, even though they read the words "lift up" or "go in," and even though the exercise described in this book is called a movement, yet they must notice carefully that this movement is neither a bodily reaching upwards nor in the body, nor is it a local movement as from one place to another. And though it is sometimes called a rest, yet they are not to think that it is the sort of rest as is stopping in a place without moving away. For the perfection of this exercise is so pure and so spiritual in itself that, when it is well and truly understood, it shall be seen to have nothing to do with any movement or any place.

It could reasonably be called a sudden change rather than a local movement. As for time, place, and body, all three must be forgotten in all spiritual exercises. So take care in this exercise that you do not take the bodily ascension of Christ as an example for straining up your imagination bodily in the time of your prayer, as though you wished to climb above the moon. For it could never be so, spiritually. Only if you were to ascend into heaven bodily, as Christ did, could you take it for an example; but no one can do that except God, as he himself bears witness when he says: "There is no man who can ascend into heaven except he who descends from heaven [cf. John 3:13], and becomes man for the love of man." And even were it possible, as it cannot be, it would only be because of the abundance of spiritual working, simply through the power of the spirit, having no connection with any bodily stretching or straining in our imagination, either up or in or on one side or on the other. So have nothing to do with such illusion. It could never be like that.

Chapter 60

The high road and the nearest way to
heaven is measured not by yards, but by
desires.

And now perhaps you will ask how this can be right. It seems to
you that you have clear evidence that heaven is upwards, because
Christ ascended there bodily upwards and sent the Holy Spirit as
he promised, coming in physical form from above in the sight of
all the disciples. And this is our belief. And so, since you have this
clear evidence, you do not see why you should not direct your
mind upwards, bodily, in time of prayer.

I answer you as well as my feebleness permits and say: since it
was so that Christ ascended bodily and thereafter sent the Holy
Spirit in physical form, it was appropriate that it should be
upwards and from above, rather than downwards and from
beneath, from behind or in front or on one side or the other. But
leaving aside what is seemly, there was no need for him to have
gone upwards rather than downwards from the point of view of
distance to be traveled. For spiritually, heaven is as close down as
up, and up as down, behind as in front, in front as behind, on
one side as on the other; so much so that whoever has a true
desire to be in heaven, then in that moment he is in heaven spiritually. For the high road and the shortest road thither is measured by desire and not by yards. And so St. Paul says about
himself and many others: "Though our bodies are now on the

earth, nevertheless our living is in heaven" [Phil. 3:20; cf. 2 Cor. 5:6–8]. By this he means their love and their desire, which spiritually is their life. And, indeed, a soul is wherever it loves, as truly as it is in the body that lives by it and to which it gives life [cf. Luke 23:42–43; John 17:24; Gal. 2:20]. So if we wish to go in spirit to heaven, we need not strain our spirit either up or down, or on one side, or on the other.

Chapter 61

All bodily things are subject to spiritual
things; it is in the order of nature that
they follow the rule of the spiritual, and
not vice versa.

Nevertheless we need to lift up our bodily eyes and hands, as to
the bodily heaven above, in which the planets are fixed. I mean,
of course, if we are moved by the work of our spirit; otherwise
not. For every bodily thing is subject to and ruled by spiritual
things, and not the contrary.

We have an example of this in the ascension of our Lord. When
the appointed time was come in which it pleased him to go to his
Father [cf. John 13:1–3], bodily in his manhood, which was
never nor ever can be separated from his Godhead, then the manhood with the body went up, in the unity of the person, mightily
through the power of the Spirit of God. It was most seemly and
fitting that this should be upwards in visible appearance.

The same subjection of the body to the spirit can truly be
understood, in a sense, in the spiritual exercise described in this
book by the experience of those who undertake it. For whenever
a soul disposes itself effectively to this exercise, then straightaway
and suddenly, and imperceptibly on the part of him who is making the exercise, the body, which perhaps before he began was a
little bent over toward one side or the other in order to be more
comfortable, comes upright by the power of the spirit, so that the

body imitates and follows the work of the spirit, which is happening spiritually; and this is very appropriate.

It is because of this seemliness that man, who is the most seemly creature in body that God ever made, is not made bent downwards to the earth like all the other animals, but upright toward heaven [cf. Eccl. 7:29]. This is because he must represent in bodily likeness the spiritual work of the soul, which must be spiritually upright and not crooked. Notice that I say spiritually, and not bodily. For how could a soul, which by nature has no bodily qualities, be strained bodily upright? No, it could not be. So take care not to interpret bodily what is meant spiritually, though it be spoken in bodily metaphor, as in these words "up" or "down," "in" or "out," "behind" or "before," "on one side" or "on the other." For no matter how spiritual a thing may be in itself, yet when we come to speak of it, since speech is a bodily exercise performed with the tongue, which is an instrument of the body, it is necessary that bodily metaphors be used. But should it on that account be interpreted and understood bodily? No, spiritually.

Chapter 62

How a man can know when his spiritual activity concerns what is beneath
him or outside himself, when it is
within him and on a par with himself,
and when it is above him and under his
God.

So that you may know how to understand spiritually words
whose literal meaning is material, I intend to explain to you the
spiritual meaning of certain words pertaining to spiritual activity. Thus you will know clearly and unmistakably when your
spiritual activity concerns what is beneath you and outside
yourself, when it concerns what is within you and on a par
with yourself, and when it concerns what is above you and
under your God.

Every kind of material thing is outside yourself and naturally
below you. Yes, the sun and the moon and all the stars, even
though they are above your body, are nevertheless below your
soul.

All angels and all saints, no matter how they are reformed by
grace or adorned with virtues and therefore above you in purity,
are nevertheless no more than equal with you by nature.

Within yourself, there are the natural powers of your soul. The
three principal are mind, reason and will; and the secondary,
imagination and sensuality.

In nature, there is nothing above you except God alone.

Wherever you read the word "yourself" in a spiritual context, this means your soul and not your body. The nature and worthiness of your work is to be judged according to the nature of the object upon which the powers of your soul are exercised, whether the object is below you, within you, or above you.

Chapter 63

Of the powers of the soul in general.
Specifically, how mind is a principal
power, containing in itself the other
powers and all their activities.

The mind is so great a power in itself that there is a sense in which it is true to say that it is never itself at work. But reason and will are two working powers, and so are imagination and sensuality. The mind contains and comprehends within itself all these four powers and their activities. The mind cannot be said to act in any way, unless this comprehension is itself activity.

I call some of the powers of the soul principal and some secondary not because the soul is divisible, for that is impossible, but because all the objects on which they are exercised are separable. And some of these objects are principal, as are all spiritual things, and some secondary, as are all material things. The two principal working powers, reason and will, work entirely by themselves with regard to all spiritual things, without the help of the two secondary powers.

With regard to material things, whether these are bodily present or absent, the imagination and sensuality work as the animals do, with the bodily senses. But it is not possible for the soul, by means of these two powers, to come to know the source of activity and mode of being of material creatures, nor the cause of their being and their creation, without the help of reason and will. It is because of this that reason and will are called principal powers; the field of their activity is purely spiritual and never material. Imagination and sensuality are called secondary, for they work in the body with bodily instruments, which are our five senses.

Mind is called a principal power because it contains in itself spiritually not only all the other powers, but also all the objects on which these powers work. Let me explain.

Chapter 64

Of the other two principal powers, reason and will, and their activity before
and after original sin.

Reason is a power by means of which we can distinguish the evil
from the good, the bad from the worse, the good from the better, the worse from the worst, the better from the best. Before
man sinned, reason could do all this naturally. But now it is so
blinded with original sin that it can do this work only if it is
enlightened by grace. Both reason itself and the object upon
which it works are comprehended and contained in the mind.

Will is a power by means of which we choose the good when
this has been ascertained by reason. Through the will we love
God, desire God, and finally come to rest in God with full liking
and full consent. Before man sinned, will could never be deceived
in its choice, in its loving or in any of its works; then it had the
natural power of appreciating everything at its true worth. But
now it can do this only if it is strengthened by grace, for very
often, because of the infection of original sin, it accepts a thing as
good when it has only the appearance of good and is really evil.
The mind contains and comprehends in itself both the will and
the object of its willing.

Chapter 65

Of the first secondary power, whose
name is imagination; its activity and its
obedience to reason, before and after
original sin.

Imagination is a power by means of which we make all our
images of things, whether they are absent or present. The imagination itself and the images it makes are contained in the mind.
Before Adam sinned, imagination was so obedient to reason—it
was, in a manner of speaking, its servant—that it never presented to reason any unseemly image of any bodily creature or
any fanciful image of any spiritual creature. But now it is not so.
Unless it is restrained by the light of grace in reason, the imagination never ceases, whether we are asleep or awake, to present
various unseemly images of bodily creatures or else some fanciful picture that is either a bodily representation of a spiritual
thing or else a spiritual representation of a bodily thing. Such
representations are always false, deceptive, and compounded
with error.

This disobedience of the imagination can clearly be seen in
those who are recently converted from the world to a life of devotion, during the time of prayer. Until their imagination is, in great
measure, controlled by the light of grace in reason, as it is in continual meditation on spiritual things (for example, on their

wretched state, on the Passion and the humanity of our Lord God, and so on), they cannot get rid of the elaborate variety of thoughts, fancies, and images that are served up and imprinted on their minds by the light and the curiosity of the imagination. All this disobedience is the painful result of original sin.

Chapter 66

The other secondary power, which is
called sensuality; its activity and its obedience to the will, before and after original sin.

The sensuality is a power of the soul whose sphere of activity is
in the bodily senses; through it we have knowledge and experience of all bodily creatures, whether they please us or not. It has
two functions: one through which it looks to our physical needs,
the other through which it ministers to the pleasures of our
senses. It is this power that complains when the body lacks what
is necessary for it and, when we are seeking what the body
needs, impels us to take more than is necessary in order to satisfy
and minister to our pleasure. It complains when we are deprived
of creatures that please us and greatly delights in the presence of
such creatures. The presence of creatures that displease it annoys
the sensuality, and it is greatly delighted by the absence of such
creatures. This power itself and the object of its working are contained in the mind.

Before man sinned, the sensuality was so obedient to the
will—it was its servant in a manner of speaking—that it never
presented the will with any inordinate pleasure in or repugnance
for bodily creatures or with any spiritual counterfeit of pleasure
or pain induced by spiritual enemies in the bodily senses. But
now it is not so. Unless it is ruled by grace in the will, so that it

can accept meekly and measurably the pain of original sin—which it experiences in the absence of pleasant things needed by the body and in the presence of unpleasant things beneficial to the spirit—and also can refrain from lusting after those pleasant and necessary things and from rejoicing excessively in the absence of those unpleasant but beneficial things, it will, in its wretchedness and wantonness, wallow like a swine in the mud in the pleasures of this world and the foul flesh; so much that all our living becomes beastly and carnal instead of being human and spiritual.

Chapter 67

Unless we know the powers of the soul
and their way of working, we may easily
be deceived in our understanding of
spiritual words and spiritual activity;
and our soul is made godlike by grace.

You can see then, my friend, into what a wretched state we are
fallen because of original sin. It is hardly surprising that we
should be like blind men and be easily deceived in our under-
standings of spiritual words and spiritual activities, particularly
those of us who are ignorant of the powers of the soul and the
way in which these powers operate.

So whenever your mind is occupied with any material thing,
no matter how good the end in view may be, you are still beneath
yourself in this working and outside yourself. And whenever you
are aware that your mind is occupied with the intricacies of the
powers of your soul and the way in which they operate in spiritual matters, such things as your own vices or virtues or those of
any spiritual creature who is on a par with you by nature, to the
end that by this activity you may learn to know yourself and
advance in perfection, then you are within yourself and on a par
with yourself. But whenever you are aware that your mind is
occupied with no created thing, whether material or spiritual, but
only with the substance of God himself, as indeed the mind is and
can be in the experience of the exercise described in this book,
then you are above yourself and under your God.

You are above yourself because you are striving by grace to reach a point to which you cannot come by nature, that is to say, to be made one with God in spirit [1 Cor. 6:17] and in love and in oneness of wills. You are beneath your God; though it can be said that during this time God and yourself are not two but one in spirit, and insofar as you or any other who experiences the perfection of this work, "because of this oneness and by witness of holy Scripture, may truly be called a god" [Ps. 82:6], nevertheless you are still beneath him. For he is God by nature from without beginning; and there was a time when you were nothing in substance, and even afterward when you were by his power and love made something, then deliberately by sin you made yourself worse than nothing. It is only by his mercy and without any merit of yours that you are made a god in grace, united with him in spirit without any division between you, both here and in the happiness of heaven without end. So though you are one with him in grace, you are yet far, far beneath him in nature.

So you can see, my friend, from what I say, at least in part, that he who is ignorant of the powers of his own soul, and the way in which these powers operate, can very easily be deceived in his understanding of words that are set down with a spiritual meaning. You can also see in some way the reason why I did not dare to bid you openly to show your desire to God, but I bade you do all that you could to hide it and to conceal it like a child. And I still do so, for fear that you should understand bodily what is meant spiritually.

Chapter 68

What is nowhere to the bodily senses is everywhere spiritually; our outward nature reckons nothing of the work of this book.

Similarly, where someone else would direct you to gather together all your powers and faculties within yourself and worship God there, I am not happy with such counsel, for fear of deceit and lest these words be taken in a bodily way, even though they are well and truly said and none more true if they are properly understood. My counsel is to take care that you are in no sense within yourself. To put it briefly, I would have you be neither outside yourself, above yourself, nor behind, nor on one side or the other.

"Where, then," you will say, "am I to be? According to your reckoning, nowhere!" Now, indeed, you speak well, for it is there that I would have you. Because nowhere bodily is everywhere spiritually. Take good care, then, that your spiritual exercise is nowhere bodily. Then, wherever the object is on which you set yourself to labor in the substance of your mind, truly you are there in spirit, as truly as your body is in the place where you dwell bodily. And though all your bodily faculties can find there nothing to feed on, because they think that what you are doing is nothing, carry on, then, with that nothing, as long as you are doing it for God's love. Do not leave off, but press on earnestly in that nothing with an alert desire in your will to have God, whom no man can know. For I tell you truly that I would rather be in this way nowhere bodily, wrestling with this blind nothing, than to have such power that I could be everywhere bodily whenever I would, happily engaged with all this "something" like a lord with his possessions.

Leave aside this everywhere and this everything, in exchange for this nowhere and this nothing. Never mind at all if your senses have no understanding of this nothing; it is for this reason that I love it so much the better. It is so worthy a thing in itself that they can have no understanding of it. This nothing can be better felt than seen; it is most obscure and dark to those who have been looking at it only for a very short while. Yet to speak more truly, a soul is more blinded in experiencing it because of the abundance of spiritual light than for any darkness or lack of bodily light. Who is he that calls it nothing? It is surely our outward man, not our inward. Our inward man calls it All [cf. 2 Cor. 6:16], for because of it he is well taught to have understanding of all things bodily or spiritual, without any specific knowledge of any one thing in itself.

Chapter 69

How a man's affections are marvelously
changed in the spiritual experience of
this nothing, which happens nowhere.

A man's affection is remarkably changed in the spiritual experience of this nothing when it is achieved nowhere. For the first time that he looks upon it, he finds there imprinted all the particular sinful acts that he ever committed since his bodily or spiritual birth, in secret or in darkness. And no matter what way he turns, they will always appear before his eyes, till such time as he shall have in great part rubbed them away with much hard labor, many sore sighings, and many bitter tears.

It seems to him, sometimes, in this labor, that to look upon it is like looking upon hell. He despairs of ever winning out of that pain to the perfection of spiritual rest. Many arrive so far inwardly, but because of the great pains that they experience and because of the absence of consolation, they go back to behold bodily things, to seek fleshly comforts without, because of the absence of spiritual consolation that they have not yet deserved and which they would have deserved if they had endured a while.

He that has patience sometimes experiences consolation and has some hope of perfection. For he feels and sees that many of the particular sins committed in the past are in great part rubbed away by the assistance of grace. But always in the midst of the consolation he feels pain; but now it seems to him that it shall have an end, for it is growing less and less. So he calls it not hell, but purgatory. Sometimes he does not find any particular sin written upon it, but it seems to him that it is a lump of sin and, somehow or other, nothing else than himself. And then it is to be called the ground and the pain of original sin. Sometimes it seems to him that it is paradise or heaven, because of the many wonderful sweetnesses and consolations, joys and blessed virtues that he finds in it. Sometimes it seems to him that it is God, because of the rest and the peace that he finds in it. But let him think what he will, he shall always find that it is a cloud of unknowing which is between him and his God.

Chapter 70

The silencing of our bodily senses leads
most readily to the experience of spiritual things; similarly, the silencing of
our spiritual faculties leads to such
experiential knowledge of God as is
possible by grace in this present life.

Work hard in this nothing and this nowhere, and desert your
outward bodily senses and the objects of their activity. For I tell
you truly that this exercise cannot be understood by them.

With your bodily eyes you cannot comprehend anything except
by its length and breadth, its smallness and greatness, its roundness and squareness, its farness and nearness, and its color; by
your ears, nothing except noise or some manner of sound; by
your nose, nothing except stench or savor; by taste, nothing except
sour or sweet, salty or fresh, bitter or pleasant; and by touch,
nothing except hot or cold, hard or tender, soft or sharp. And truly
neither God nor spiritual things have any of these qualities or
quantities. So leave your outward senses and do not work with
them, neither exteriorly nor interiorly. For all those who set themselves to be spiritual workers inwardly and yet think that they
ought either to hear, smell, see, taste, or touch spiritual things,
either within or outside themselves, surely are deceived and are
working wrongly, against the course of nature. For by nature it is
ordained that through the bodily senses men should have know-

ledge of all outward bodily things, and not that they should come to the knowledge of ghostly things through them.

I am speaking of their positive activity. For we can come to the knowledge of spiritual things through their lack of activity. When, for example, we read or hear of certain things and realize that our bodily senses cannot inform us what these things are through their qualities, then we can certainly be assured that these things are spiritual and not bodily things.

The same is true spiritually of our spiritual powers, when we are laboring concerning the knowledge of God himself. For no matter how much spiritual understanding a man may have in the knowledge of all created spiritual things, he can never, by the work of his understanding, arrive at the knowledge of an uncreated spiritual thing, which is nothing except God. But by the failing of it, he can. For where his understanding fails is in nothing except God alone; and it was for this reason that St. Denis said, "The truly divine knowledge of God is that which is known by unknowing." And now whoever cares to examine the works of Denis will find that his words clearly corroborate all that I have said or am going to say, from the beginning of this treatise to the end. But I have no mind to cite him to support my views on any other thing than this, at this moment, or any other doctor either. For at one time men believed that it was humility to say nothing out of their own heads unless they corroborated it by Scripture and the sayings of the fathers. But now this practice indicates nothing except cleverness and a display of erudition. You do not need it, and so I am not going to do it. He who has ears, let him hear [Matt. 13:9]; and he who is moved to believe it, let him do so; otherwise he will not.

Chapter 71

Some may experience the perfection of
this exercise during rapture, but some
can experience it whenever they will, in
their normal conscious state.

Some people believe that this work is so difficult and so awesome
that they say it cannot be undertaken without great toil preceding
it, that it can be achieved only very seldom, and this during the
time of rapture. To these I wish to answer as well as my feebleness permits. I say that it depends on the ordinance and the disposition of God and the spiritual capacity of those to whom this
grace of contemplation and spiritual working is given. There are
some who cannot reach it without long and frequent spiritual
exercises, and even then it is only very seldom that they will
experience the perfection of this exercise, at the special calling of
our Lord; this is what is meant by rapture.

But there are some who are so refined by grace and in spirit
and so familiar with God in this grace of contemplation, that they
may have the perfection of it whenever they will, in their ordinary
state of soul, whether they are sitting, walking, standing, or kneeling. And at the same time they have the full command of all their
faculties, bodily and spiritual, and can use them if they so wish—
not without a certain hindrance, but one not hard to overcome.
We have an example of the first type in Moses and of the second
in Aaron, the priest of the Temple [cf. Exod. 24:15ff.].

This grace of contemplation is prefigured by the ark of the testament in the Old Law; and those who exercise themselves in this grace are prefigured by those who are most concerned with this ark, as the story bears witness. This work and this grace is rightly said to resemble that ark. For just as in that ark all the jewels and relics of the Temple were contained, in the same way in this little love, when it is offered, are contained all the virtues of a man's soul, which is the spiritual temple of God.

Before Moses could come to see this ark and to know how it had to be made, he climbed up to the top of the mountain and dwelt there and worked in a cloud for six days with hard and long labor, until the seventh day, when our Lord would deign to show him the way in which the ark should be made. By the long labor of Moses and the delay in the revelation to him, we are to understand those who cannot come to the perfection of this spiritual exercise unless long labor precedes it, and even then only very seldom and when God will deign to show it.

But what Moses could only come to see very seldom, Aaron, because of his office, had in his power to see in the Temple within the veil as often as it pleased him to enter. By Aaron's power we are to understand all those of whom I spoke above, those who by their spiritual skill and the help of grace can make the perfection of this exercise their own as often as it pleases them.

Chapter 72

He who habitually practices this exercise must not take it for granted that other contemplatives have his precise experience.

You can see, then, that the man who can only come to see and experience the perfection of this work with heavy toil, and even then only seldom, can easily be deceived if he speaks, thinks, and judges of other men according to his own experience: that they too cannot come to it except seldom and only then with hard labor. Similarly, he also can be deceived who has it whenever he wishes, if he judges all others by his own experience and says that they can have it when they wish. Forget this, for certainly no one must think in this way. If such be God's pleasure, it may be that those who at first can have it only seldom and even then at great cost may later on come to have it when they will and as often as they like. We have an example of this in Moses. On the mountain he saw the form of the ark very rarely and after heavy toil. But later on, within the veil, he saw it as often as it pleased him [cf. Exod. 33:7–11].

Chapter 73

This grace of contemplation is prefigured in the ark of the covenant, in the
sense that Moses, Beseleel, and Aaron, in
their dealings with the ark, are three
types of how we exercise ourselves in
this grace.

There were three men who were chiefly concerned with this ark
of the Old Testament: Moses, Beseleel, and Aaron. Moses was
taught how it should be made on the mountain of our Lord [cf.
Exod. 25:7–27:21]. Beseleel fashioned and made it in the valley
according to the directions which were revealed on the mountain [cf. Exod. 36:1–38:31]. Aaron had it in his keeping in the
Temple, to touch it and see it as often as it pleased him.

According to the example of these three, we make progress in
this grace of contemplation in three ways. Sometimes we make
progress by grace alone, and then we are like Moses, who, for all
the hard cost of the mountain climb, could only come to see it
seldom; and that sight was only through the revelation of our
Lord, when it pleased him to show it and not as a reward which
Moses deserved. Sometimes we make progress in this grace by
our own spiritual skill, supported by grace; and then we are like
Beseleel, who could not see the ark before he had fashioned it
with his own skill, helped by the pattern which was revealed to
Moses on the mountain. And sometimes we make progress in

this grace by other men's teaching; and then we are like Aaron, who had it in his keeping and could regularly see and touch the ark whenever he liked, after Beseleel had fashioned and made it ready for him.

So, my spiritual friend, though I am a wretch, unworthy to teach any creature, in this exercise I hold the office of Beseleel. Perhaps I am speaking childishly and foolishly, for in a way I am fashioning and making plain on your behalf the nature of this spiritual ark. But you can work far better and much more worthily than I do, if you will take on the office of Aaron, that is to say, to exercise yourself continuously in it for yourself and for me as well. Do so, I beseech you, for the love of God Almighty. And since we are both called by God to work in this exercise, I beseech you, for God's love, to fill up on your part what is wanting in mine [cf. Col. 1:24].

Chapter 74

A man is rightly disposed to the contemplation which is the subject matter
of this book when he cannot read or
speak about it, or hear it read or spoken
about, without feeling that he is really
suited to this work and its effects; a rep-
etition of the directives given in the
prologue.

But if you think that this way of working is not according to
your bodily or spiritual disposition, you can leave it and take
another safely and without reproach, as long as it is with good
spiritual counsel. And in that case I beseech you that you will
hold me excused. For truly my purpose in writing this book was
to help you to make progress according to my own simple
knowledge. That was my intention. So read it over two or three
times; the oftener, the better, and the more you shall understand
of it; so that, perhaps, if some sentence was very difficult for you
to understand at the first or second reading, it will then seem to
you easy enough.

Yes, indeed. It seems impossible to my understanding that any
soul who is disposed for this exercise should read the book, privately or aloud, without feeling during that time a true affinity
for the effect of this exercise. So if it seems to you that it does you
good, thank God heartily, and for God's love pray for me.

Do this, then. I also pray you, for God's love, not to let anyone examine this book except those whom you believe to be disposed for it—as you find written at the beginning of the book, where it says what men may undertake this exercise and when they should do so. And if you do let any such person examine it, then I beg you to bid them take the necessary time to examine it right through. For it may happen that some question occurs at the beginning or in the middle which depends on what follows and is not fully explained in that place. If it is not explained here, it will be so a little later on, or else at the end. Hence, if a man were to read one section and not another, it might easily happen that he would fall into error. So I beg you to do as I say. If you think that there is any point here that you would wish to have clarified in greater detail than it is, let me know what it is and what you think about it, and I shall amend it to the best of my simple ability.

But as for the chatterboxes, the rumormongers, the gossips, the tittle-tattlers, the faultfinders of every sort, I would not want them to see this book. It was never my intention to write on these matters for them. I would refuse to have them interfering with it, those clever clerics, or layfolk either. For no matter how excellent they may be in matters pertaining to the active life, my subject is not for them.

Chapter 75

Of definite signs whereby a man may
test whether or not one is called by God
to take up this exercise.

All those who read the subject matter of this book, or listen to it
read or spoken about, and in their reading or listening think that
this is good and congenial to them are not on that account called
by God to undertake this exercise simply because of this congenial feeling that they have in the time of their reading. It can happen that this feeling comes more from a natural intellectual
curiosity than from any calling of grace.

   If, however, they wish to discover whence this feeling comes,
they can find out in this way if they so wish. First, let them see
to it that they have first done all that in them lies to prepare
themselves for it by the cleansing of their conscience according
to the judgment of the holy church and with the approval of
their spiritual director. So far, so good. But if they wish to know
more, let them see if this impulse is always pressing on their
minds more regularly than is so with any other spiritual exercise. And if it seems to them that nothing that they do, bodily
or spiritually, is of any value according to the witness of their
conscience except this little secret love, directed in a spiritual
way as the chief of all their exercises. If that is their feeling,
then it is a token that they are called by God to this exercise;
otherwise, not.

I do not say, for those who are called to undertake this exercise, that this stirring will always exist and dwell in their minds continuously. No, it is not so. For often the actual experience of this impulse is withdrawn for various reasons from the young spiritual apprentice in this exercise, sometimes in order that he might not become too familiar with it and so consider that it is for the most part in his own power to have it when he pleases and as he pleases. Such a belief would be pride. Whenever the experience of this grace is withdrawn, pride is the cause. That is to say, not actual pride, but the pride that would be there unless this experience of grace were withdrawn. And often young people in their folly think that God is their enemy when he is their best friend.

Sometimes the experience is withdrawn because of their carelessness; when this happens, they experience immediately a very sharp pain that afflicts them very sorely. Sometimes our Lord deliberately delays the experience, because it is his will, by such delaying, to enlarge the experience and make one care more for it when it is found again and experienced afresh after having been lost for a long time. This is one of the clearest and simplest signs that a soul can have to know whether he is called to undertake this exercise or not: if he feels, after such a delay and a long absence of this experience, when it comes suddenly, as it does, achieved without any intermediary, that he has a greater fervor of desire and a greater longing to get on with this exercise than he ever had before; so much so that often, I believe, he has more joy in the finding of it than ever he had sorrow in the losing of it. If it is thus, then it is truly a most authentic token that he is called by God to undertake this exercise, whatever his state is or has been.

Because it is not what you are or what you have been that God looks at with his merciful eyes, but what you desire to be. And St. Gregory is witness that "All holy desires grow by delay; and if they diminish by delay, then they were never holy desires." And he who experiences less and less joy in the new experiences and sudden presentations of his own desires, though they all must be called natural desires for the good, nevertheless they were never holy desires. Of this holy desire St. Augustine speaks, when he says that "the whole of life of good Christian men is nothing else but holy desires."

Farewell, spiritual friend, in God's blessing and mine. And I beseech almighty God that true peace, sane counsel, and spiritual comfort in God with abundance of grace always be with you, and with all those who on earth love God.

Amen.

ABOUT THE EDITOR

HarperCollins Spiritual Classics Series Editor Emilie Griffin has long been interested in the classics of the devotional life. She has written a number of books on spiritual formation and transformation, including *Clinging: The Experience of Prayer* and *Wilderness Time: A Guide to Spiritual Retreat*. With Richard J. Foster she coedited *Spiritual Classics: Selected Readings on the Twelve Spiritual Disciplines*. Her latest book is *Wonderful and Dark Is this Road: Discovering the Mystic Path*. She is a board member of Renovaré and leads retreats and workshops throughout the United States. She and her husband, William, live in Alexandria, Louisiana.

THE CLASSICS OF **WESTERN SPIRITUALITY**
A LIBRARY OF THE GREAT SPIRITUAL MASTERS

These volumes contain original writings of universally acknowledged teachers within the Catholic, Protestant, Eastern Orthodox, Jewish, Islamic, and American Indian traditions.

The Classics of Western Spirituality unquestionably provide the most in-depth, comprehensive, and accessible panorama of Western mysticism ever attempted. From the outset, the Classics has insisted on the highest standards for these volumes, including new translations from the original languages, and helpful introductions and other aids by internationally recognized scholars and religious thinkers, designed to help the modern reader to come to a better appreciation of these works that have nourished the three monotheistic faiths for centuries.

The Cloud of Unknowing
Edited and Introduced
by James Walsh
0-8091-2332-0 $22.95

Teresa of Avila
Edited and Introduced
by Kieran Kavanaugh, O.C.D.
0-8091-2254-5 $22.95

John of the Cross
Edited and Introduced
by Kieran Kavanaugh, O.C.D.
0-8091-2839-X $21.95

John and Charles Wesley
Edited and Introduced
by Frank Whaling
0-8091-2368-1 $26.95

For more information on the
CLASSICS OF WESTERN SPIRITUALITY, contact Paulist Press
(800) 218-1903 • www.paulistpress.com